THE GABBITAS

TOP 500

INDEPENDENT

SCHOOLS

WITHDRAWN

THE GABBITAS
TOP 500
INDEPENDENT
SCHOOLS

Gabbitas Education
CONSULTANTS SINCE 1873

The global experts in British independent education

KoganPage

LONDON PHILADELPHIA NEW DELHI

Publisher's note

Every possible effort has been made to ensure that the information contained in this book is accurate at the time of going to press, and the publishers and author cannot accept responsibility for any errors or omissions, however caused. No responsibility for loss or damage occasioned to any person acting, or refraining from action, as a result of the material in this publication can be accepted by the editor, the publisher or the author.

First published in Great Britain and the United States in 2014 by Kogan Page Limited

2nd Floor, 45 Gee Street
London EC1V 3RS
United Kingdom
www.koganpage.com

1518 Walnut Street, Suite 1100
Philadelphia PA 19102
USA

4737/23 Ansari Road
Daryaganj
New Delhi 110002
India

© Gabbitas, 2014

ISBN   978 0 7494 7035 7
E-ISBN   978 0 7494 7036 4

British Library Cataloguing-in-Publication Data

A CIP record for this book is available from the British Library.

Typeset by Graphicraft Limited, Hong Kong
Printed and bound in Great Britain by Henry Ling Ltd, Dorchester

CONTENTS

INTRODUCTION

In the past 18 months I have had the good fortune to visit more than a few independent schools and, as I've experienced throughout my career as a head and teacher, I regularly leave the premises thoroughly impressed by the educationalists there, who really are the sum of this wonderful sector. Many schools are able to inspire and instil in their pupils a wonderful sense of the value of academic education, and a self worth that equips them with the skills to embrace and create opportunities out of every twist and turn that life throws at them. However, the education provided at these schools is much, much more than just the academic; children educated in the British independent sector also complete their school years with poise, manners, confidence, and an almost famous sense of fair play, honour and humour that is respected worldwide. These pupils truly are the ambassadors for 'British Education PLC', which now spans the Globe providing education that is the envy of many nations.

The Gabbitas Top 500 Independent Schools is a definitive selection of leading preparatory and senior schools in the UK. The schools have been chosen by a diverse range of education professionals, including heads past and present, consultants and representatives from independent school organisations. Given the quality of UK independent schools this task has been monumentally difficult and the cause of not a few differences of opinion.

The Top 500 is a selection we at Gabbitas are proud of because of the wide range of factors taken into consideration including the educational provision, pastoral care, teaching and ethos of a school. Inclusion is not based solely on how many A/A* grade passes a school achieves, as detailed in the league tables. Some of the schools in this book are, however, highly academic and rightly proud of this reputation, but also selected are those that suit the less academic pupils; paying close attention to a wide range of opportunities and ensuring that all flourish in later life with a full complement of social skills and flair.

Gabbitas has been in the education business since 1873. Whether finding the best and most suitable headmaster for a school in the UK or overseas, a nursery support assistant at a local Kindergarten or finding the perfect boarding school for bright UK and international students – our consultants are here to support and work with families and schools.

Independent education is a top priority for families the world over wishing to provide the very best for their children. In this book, as well as the unique schools that comprise the UK independent sector, we also focus on the exciting development of international schools overseas and the excellent education they provide for internationally mobile families.

I hope that you enjoy and benefit from the insight we provide into the top Independent Schools here in the UK and the range of highlighted British curriculum schools around the world.

Yours sincerely

Ian Hunt, Managing Director Gabbitas

THE GABBITAS
TOP 500

The Gabbitas Top 500 Independent Schools is a guide to the finest schools of the British independent education sector. We do say 'sector' but by their very nature the top schools often are individual with unique characters and histories, offering a very distinctive educational experience for their pupils.

The guide is divided into three main sections: Senior Schools, Preparatory Schools and International Schools. Each section has a full listing of selected schools and school profiles. To help readers gain their bearings, there is a regional index at the end of each section, grouping schools by location.

Senior schools

The Top 300 senior schools in the UK are presented first of all, in alphabetical order. Included amongst these are as you would expect, top public schools, boarding schools, day schools, and single sex schools. There are seniors only accepting pupils from 11 or 13 and also those with prep and sometimes pre-prep departments. Whether a *stand-alone* senior or a *straight-through* school, in this section, focus is squarely on senior provision.

Preparatory schools

A select group of 200 preps is introduced by our consultants in the next section. Schools from around the UK are included, all of which provide an exceptional education for preparatory pupils, whilst paving the way for senior school entry.

Highlighted international schools

Exactly one hundred international schools is the subject of this part of the guide. Colin Bell, CEO of the Council of British International Schools introduces readers to highlighted schools teaching British curriculum, IB or other curricula taught in English. Readers are invited to consider schools throughout the world including those based in the Americas, those in the Far East, and also noteworthy schools throughout the Middle East and Europe.

Before introducing the Top Schools themselves, we offer insight for parents based overseas wishing to send their children to school in the UK. We also provide, as a useful reference, details of the examinations and qualifications found at these schools.

CONSIDERATIONS FOR PARENTS BASED OVERSEAS

The increasing number of children with parents overseas attending UK independent schools suggests that the British educational *export* is growing in popularity worldwide. According to the most recent independent schools council census there were 25,441 non-British pupils in the independent sector, an average of over 20 per school.

Choosing a school in another country throws up a range of additional considerations and the best advice is to plan ahead as far as possible – at least a year in advance. This will allow time to research all the options fully before making an informed choice. There are quite a few things to prepare for initially including English language teaching and support, admissions procedures and academic considerations such as course choices. Also vitally important are the practicalities of boarding provision and support for international students outside school and term time.

Level of English

Top independent schools will generally expect your child to arrive with a good standard of English to enable full access to the curriculum. Additional in-school tuition is sometimes available to improve fluency and accuracy, but you will need to check with any school you are interested in well before applying. Some of the top boarding schools have international study centres, where international students can often develop their English language capabilities alongside academic studies. Those in *The Gabbitas Top 500* with, or with links to, a study centre include:

- Bedford School, Befordshire
- Boxhill, Surrey
- Sherbourne School, Dorset
- Kent College Canterbury, Kent
- King's Ely, Cambridgeshire
- Millfield School, Somerset
- Moreton Hall, Shropshire
- Rossall School, Lancashire
- Taunton School, Somerset

Another option for families worried about their child's linguistic ability is to arrange a summer at one of the UK's many language schools before joining in September.

Academic background

If your child has been educated within the British system, it should not be difficult to join a school in the UK, although care should be taken to avoid changing schools while a student is in the middle of GCSE or A level studies. However, if your child has not been following a British curriculum, entry to a mainstream independent school may be less straightforward. The younger your child, the easier it is likely to be for him or her to adapt to a new school environment. Prep schools may accept overseas pupils at any stage up to the final two years, when pupils are prepared for Common Entrance exams and entry may be more difficult. Senior schools in particular, will normally look for evidence of ability and achievement comparable with pupils educated in the British system and will probably wish to test your child in English, Maths and Science before deciding whether to offer a place. Students wishing to enter the Sixth Form will probably be tested in the subjects they wish to study. Recent reports and transcripts, in translation, are also generally required by schools.

If your child has been following the International Baccalaureate (IB) programme overseas and you would like to continue studies in the UK it is generally advisable to seek a school offering the same qualification. As the IB is increasingly available in the UK, you will find a number of top schools offering the qualification including Cheltenham Ladies' College, Pangbourne, Marlborough and North London Collegiate to name but a few.

Top boarding schools: location

If you are looking for a boarding school, your geographical horizons can be much wider than those of parents only considering day places. Most schools, including those in the beautiful countryside of rural England, are within easy reach of major transport links and the UK is well served by air, rail and road routes. In addition schools generally make arrangements to have your child escorted between school and the airport and vice versa – so it's possible to consider top schools whether in Somerset, the Home Counties or Edinburgh for example.

Visiting top schools

Once you have decided on the most suitable type of school, you can obtain information on specific schools. It is essential that you visit schools before making a final choice. Try to plan your visits during term time.

Independent schools set their own holidays and term dates, making it difficult to give a definitive schedule for the year at all schools. As a general guide, the academic year is divided into three terms *autumn* (Sept), *spring* (Jan) and *summer* (Apr) each with a half term holiday. A generous, six-week-long holiday follows the summer term.

Questions to ask top schools

English language support
What level of English does the school expect? Is additional support available at school? How is this organised? Is there a qualified English language teacher?

Pupil mix
How many other pupils of my and other nationalities attend the school and what arrangements are made to encourage them to mix with English pupils?

Pastoral care
If your child has special dietary needs or is required to observe specific religious principles, is the school willing and able to cope? Would your child also be expected to take part in the school's normal worship?

Ask about arrangements for escorting your child to and from school at the beginning and end of term. Some schools have a minibus service to take children to railway stations and airports or will arrange a taxi where appropriate.

Guardianship

Ask schools about their policies on guardian families. Most schools insist that boarding pupils whose parents live overseas have an appointed guardian living near the school who can offer a home for 'exeats' (weekends out of school), half-term breaks and at the beginning and end of term in case flights do not coincide exactly with school dates. A guardian may be a relative or friend appointed by parents, but it should be remembered that the arrangement may need to continue for some years and that guardianship is a substantial commitment.

Making guardianship arrangements

For parents with no suitable contacts in the UK, schools may be able to assist in making guardianship arrangements. Alternatively there are independent organisations, including Gabbitas, which offer expertise in this area. Good guardian families should offer a 'home from home', looking after the interests and welfare of your child as they would their own, providing a separate room and space for study, attending school events and parents' evenings, involving your child in all aspects of family life and encouraging him or her to feel comfortable and relaxed while away from school. Some guardianship organisations are very experienced in selecting suitable families who will offer a safe and happy home to students a long way from their own parents. The range of services offered and fees charged by different providers will vary, but you should certainly look for a service that offers the following:

- Personally ensures that families are visited in their homes by an experienced member of staff and that all appropriate checks are made;
- Takes a genuine interest in your child's educational and social welfare and progress;
- Keeps in touch with you, your child, the school and the guardian family to ensure that all is running smoothly;
- Provides administrative support as required and assistance with visa and travel requirements, medical and dental checks and insurance, and any other matters such as the purchase of school uniform, sports kit and casual clothes.

AEGIS accredited guardianship

Parents seeking a guardianship provider may like to contact AEGIS (the Association for the Education and Guardianship of International Students), of which Gabbitas is a founder member. The purpose of AEGIS is to promote best practice in all areas of guardianship and to safeguard the welfare and happiness of overseas children attending educational institutions in the UK. AEGIS aims to provide accreditation for all reputable guardianship organisations. Applicants for membership are required to undergo assessment and inspection to ensure that they are adhering to the AEGIS Code of Practice and fulfilling the Membership Criteria before full membership can be granted. For further details contact Gabbitas Guardianship on +44 (0)20 7734 0161 or visit www.gabbitas.co.uk. For further information about AEGIS, visit the website at www.aegisuk.net.

Preparing your child to come to the UK

Coming to school in a different country is an enriching and exciting experience. You can help your child to settle in more quickly by encouraging him or her to take a positive approach and to absorb the traditions and social customs of school and family life in the UK. After the first year, most children begin to feel more confident and comfortable in their surroundings, both at school and with their guardian family.

Where to go for help

You may be able to obtain information about schools from official sources in your own country. For detailed guidance and assistance in the UK you may wish to contact an independent educational consultancy such as Gabbitas for advice on all aspects of education in the UK and transferring into the British system.

EXAMINATIONS AND QUALIFICATIONS

Top schools in the independent sector are well known for their innovative approaches to education. This is reflected in how they have helped shape the qualifications landscape of the UK not to mention further afield. The IB, IGCSE and Cambridge Pre U were, for example, initially established in the UK, in the independent sector. With greater freedoms to devise curricula and to examine academic performance, top independent schools are often quick to introduce and try new methods.

As some of the top schools have selective entry policies, we begin with the senior school entry examination – Common Entrance (CE). Attention then moves to senior school courses and qualifications ranging from GCSE and IGCSE, to A levels, the IB and other sixth form options.

Common Entrance (CE)

The Common Entrance examination forms the basis of entry to most independent senior schools, although some schools set their own entrance exams. Traditionally it is taken by boys at the age of 13 and by girls at the age of 11. However, with the growth of co-education at senior level the divisions have become less sharply defined and the examinations are open to both boys and girls.

The Common Entrance papers are set centrally by the Independent Schools Examinations Board. The papers are marked, however, by the individual schools, which have their own marking schemes and set their own entry standards. Common Entrance is not an exam which candidates pass by reaching a national standard, rather it is used by senior schools to compare candidates and assess ability.

The content of the Common Entrance papers has undergone regular review and the Independent Schools Examinations Board has adapted syllabuses to bring them into line with curriculum requirements.

Candidates are entered by their junior or preparatory schools. Parents whose children attend state schools should apply to the Independent School Examinations Board, ideally four months before the scheduled examination date. Some pupils may need additional coaching for the exam if they are not attending an independent preparatory school. To be eligible, pupils must normally have been offered a place by a senior school subject to their performance in the exam. Pupils applying for scholarships may be required to pass Common Entrance before sitting the scholarship exam. Candidates normally take the exam in their own junior or preparatory school.

At 11+ the Common Entrance exam consists of papers in English, Mathematics and Science, and is designed to be suitable for all pupils. Most pupils who take the exam at 13+ come from independent preparatory schools. Subjects are English, Mathematics, Science (these are compulsory); French, History, Geography, Religious Studies, German, Spanish, Latin and Greek (these are optional).

The examination for 13+ entry takes place in January and May/June. For entry at 11+ the exam is held in January.

Further information on Common Entrance can be obtained from:

The General Secretary
Independent Schools Examinations Board
The Pump House
16 Queen's Avenue
Christchurch BH23 1BZ
Tel: +44 (0) 1202 487538
Fax: +44 (0) 1202 473728
E-mail: enquiries@iseb.co.uk

General Certificate of Secondary Education (GCSE)

The GCSE forms the principal course for senior school pupils aged between 14 and 16 years of age. Pupils are generally required to choose GCSE subjects in year nine before commencing their studies in year ten at age 14. Most pupils of average ability take nine or ten GCSEs including Mathematics, English and Science, although some may take eleven or more. Most GCSE courses are taught over two years but very able pupils may take some GCSE examinations after one year.

GCSE (Short Course) qualifications are also available and take only half the study time of a full GCSE. These courses are graded on the same scale as a full GCSE covering fewer topics and are equivalent to half. The GCSE (Short Course) can be used in various ways: to offer able students additional choices such as a second modern language or to offer a subject which could not otherwise be studied as a full GCSE because of other subject choices. It may also be attractive to students who need extra time in their studies and would be better suited to a two-year course devoted to a GCSE (Short Course) rather than a full GCSE.

All results for GCSE are graded on a scale from A* to G. Examinations generally have differentiated or tiered papers that target different ability ranges within the A*–G grade range. Many large-entry GCSE subjects are examined through a foundation tier covering grades C–G and a higher tier covering grades A*–D.

A review of the GCSE led to changes in the assessment system affecting both course work and examinations. Course work is replaced by controlled assessment in most subjects and external examination questions are revised. Controlled assessment was introduced to provide greater control in three areas: setting of tasks, task taking and task marking. Assessed task taking, for example, is carried out in a supervised environment such as the classroom to safeguard against plagiarism and undue assistance. External examinations now incorporate a number of different question styles to enable students to better demonstrate their knowledge, understanding and ability.

International General Certificate of Secondary Education (IGCSE)

The International General Certificate of Secondary Education (IGCSE) was originally developed for use by international schools. However, IGCSEs have since been adopted by many independent schools in the UK because of the greater flexibility and rigour offered in assessment.

The IGCSE, which is marked on the same A*–G scale as the GCSE, is widely recognised by schools, universities and employers as equivalent, and provides progression to AS and A level study in the same way. There are, however, some differences in the content and examination of the two qualifications, which vary by subject.

There are two awarding bodies for IGCSEs: University of Cambridge International Examinations (CIE), which has been awarding the qualifications for over 20 years; and Edexcel which began to award IGCSEs more recently. In addition to the differences between the IGCSE and GCSE, the content and assessment structure of the CIE and Edexcel IGCSE also vary by subject. Please contact these organisations for further information.

University of Cambridge International Examinations
1 Hills Road Cambridge CB1 2EU
United Kingdom
Tel: +44 (0) 1223 553554
Fax: +44 (0) 1223 553558

Edexcel International
One90 High Holborn London WC1V 7BH United Kingdom
Tel: +44 (0) 1204 770696
Fax: +44 (0) 2071 905700

GCE A Levels and GCE AS Levels

Advanced and Advanced Subsidiary Levels are the post-16 qualifications most widely taught in UK sixth forms and tutorial colleges. A and AS levels, as they are commonly known, are also the most prevalent means of entry to Higher Education in the UK. Subjects offered include academic studies such as Mathematics, English Literature, Physics and Geography. Vocationally focused 'Applied A levels' are also available in subjects ranging from Art and Design to Business Studies.

A level subjects are generally taught over two years, typically with two units studied in the first year and a further two in the second (although most now have four modules – some do remain with six units). The first year units make up an Advanced Subsidiary (AS) course. If these are followed in the second year by the appropriate number of A2 units (these are at a higher level than the AS units), the AS and A2 units combined represent a complete A level course.

Students may take four or five AS level subjects in the first year, with the option of reducing the number to three or four A2 subjects in the second year. Advanced

Subsidiary units focus on material appropriate for the first year of an A level course and are assessed accordingly. Second year A2 modules are more demanding and are assessed at full A level standard.

Overall assessment is based on examinations and/or coursework and may be made at stages during the course (modular) or at the end of the course (linear). A synoptic component is also incorporated into these assessments to examine students' understanding of the course as a whole and the connections between its different elements.

An A level grade is reached by combining AS and A2 grades. AS and A levels also attract UCAS (University and Colleges Admission Service) tariff points for the purpose of university entry. Students who successfully complete the first year units will be awarded an AS level. This is a qualification in its own right, although it is not enough to gain entry to university.

Passes at AS and A levels are initially graded on a scale of A to E, with the U grade (unclassified) indicating a fail. An A* is now awarded for the achievement of an A grade overall with a score of at least 90 per cent, according to the Uniform Mark Scale, in the A2 units studied.

An optional extended project is available, which gives students the opportunity to undertake individual study in a subject of their own choosing in addition to their A level courses. The extended project is a single piece of work, requiring a high degree of planning, preparation, research and autonomous working. It is assessed at the same level as A level but is equivalent to half an A level. The extended project is also graded from A* to E and for university entrance attracts half the UCAS tariff points of an A level.

The AQA Baccalaureate (AQA Bacc)

The AQA Baccalaureate (AQA Bacc) is a qualification that recognises and celebrates the achievements of well-rounded students with A levels and more. Students build on core A level subjects, adding value through wider learning and enrichment activities.

The Bacc comprises: three A level subjects (students' main subject choices), independent learning through the Extended Project Qualification, personal development through Enrichment Activities such as work-related learning, community participation and personal development. Added breadth is provided as part of the AQA Bacc course through the study of an AS level in General Studies, Critical Thinking, Citizenship or Science in Society.

Cambridge Pre-University Diploma

The Cambridge Pre-U Diploma is a new post-16 qualification developed by University of Cambridge International Examinations in collaboration with schools and universities. The qualification is designed to prepare students with the skills and knowledge required for successful progression to higher education.

More recently accredited for use within the national qualifications framework, the Cambridge Pre-U is being offered at an increasing minority of senior schools. Schools generally offer the Cambridge Pre-U alongside A levels. Within the structure of the qualification it is possible to exchange up to two A levels for corresponding Principal Subjects.

The qualification offers opportunities for interdisciplinary study, includes independent research that builds on individual subject specialisms and is informed by an international perspective. Students are able to choose from a total of 26 Principal Subjects. To qualify for the Cambridge Pre-U Diploma, students must achieve passes in at least three Principal Subjects, an Independent Research Report and a Global Perspectives Portfolio.

Cambridge Pre-U is underpinned by the following educational aims:

- Encouraging the development of well-informed, open and independent minded individuals.

- Promoting deep understanding through subject specialisation, with a depth and rigour appropriate to progression to higher education.

- Helping learners to acquire specific skills of problem-solving, critical thinking, creativity, team-working, independent learning and effective communication.

- Recognizing a wide range of individual talents and interests.

- Promoting an international outlook and cross-cultural awareness.

The structure of the qualification is linear, with one set of examinations at the end of the two-year course. Achievement is reported on a scale of nine grades: D1 (Distinction 1), D2, D3, M1 (Merit 1), M2, M3, P1 (Pass 1), P2, P3. The grade D1 reports achievement above the A level A* grade (see GCE A levels and GCE Advanced Subsidiary). The intention is to enable greater differentiation between students, especially at the higher end of the grading scale.

University of Cambridge International Examinations
1 Hills Road Cambridge CB1 2EU
Tel: +44 (0) 1223 553554
E-mail: international@cie.org.uk

The International Baccalaureate (Information supplied by the International Baccalaureate)

The International Baccalaureate is a non-profit, international educational foundation registered in Switzerland that was established in 1968. The Diploma Programme, for which the IB is best known, was developed by a group of schools seeking to establish a common curriculum and a university-entry credential for geographically mobile students. They believed that an education that emphasised critical thinking and exposure to a variety of points of view would encourage inter-cultural under-standing and acceptance of others by young people. They designed a comprehen-sive curriculum for the last two years of secondary school that could be administered in any country and that would be recognised by universities worldwide.

Today the IB offers three programmes to schools. The Diploma Programme is for students aged 16 to 19 in the final two years of secondary school. The Middle Years Programme, adopted in 1994, is for students aged 11 to 16. The Primary Years Programme, adopted in 1997, is for students aged 3 to 12. The IB has 2,400 authorised schools in 129 countries. This number is fairly evenly divided between state and private schools (including international) schools.

The Diploma Programme

The Diploma Programme (DP), for students aged 16 to 19, is a two-year course of study. Recognised internationally as a qualification for university entrance, it also allows students to fulfil the requirements of their national education system. Students share an educational experience that emphasises critical thinking as well as inter-cultural understanding and respect for others in the global community.

The DP offers a broad and balanced curriculum in which students are encour-aged to apply what they learn in the classroom to real-world issues and problems. Wherever possible, subjects are taught from an international perspective. In economics, for example, students look at economic systems from around the world. Students study six courses (including both the sciences and the human-ities) selected from the following six subject groups:

Group 1   language A1
Group 2   (second language) language ab initio, language B, language A2, and classical languages
Group 3   individuals and societies
Group 4   experimental sciences
Group 5   mathematics and computer science
Group 6   the arts

Students must also submit an extended essay, follow a course in theory of knowledge (TOK) and take part in activities to complete the creativity, action and service (CAS) requirement.

The assessment of student work in the DP is largely external. At the end of the course, students take examinations that are marked by external examiners who work closely with the IB. The types of questions asked in the examination papers include multiple-choice questions, essay questions, data-analysis questions and case studies. Students are also graded on the extended essay and on an essay and oral presentation for the TOK course.

A smaller part of the assessment of student work is carried out within schools by DP teachers. The work that is assessed includes oral commentaries in the languages, practical experimental work in the sciences, fieldwork and investigations in the humanities, and exhibitions and performances in the arts. Examiners check the assessment of samples of work from each school to ensure that IB standards are consistently applied. For each examination session, approximately 80 per cent of DP students are awarded the Diploma. The majority of students register for the Diploma, but students may also register for a limited number of Diploma subjects, for each of which they are awarded a certificate with the final grade.

The Middle Years Programme (MYP)

The Middle Years Programme (MYP), for students aged 11 to 16, recognises that students in this age group are particularly sensitive to social and cultural influences and are struggling to define themselves and their relationships to others. The programme helps students develop the skills to cope with this period of uncertainty. It encourages them to think critically and independently, to work collaboratively and to take a disciplined approach to studying. The aim of the MYP is to give students an international perspective to help them become informed about the experiences of people and cultures throughout the world. It also fosters a commitment to help others and to act as a responsible member of the community at the local, national and international levels.

Students in the MYP study all the major disciplines, including languages, humanities, sciences, mathematics, arts, technology and physical education. Each of the disciplines or 'subject groups' is studied through five areas of interaction:

- approaches to learning;
- community and service;
- human ingenuity;

- environment;
- health and social education.

The framework is flexible enough to allow a school to include subjects that are not part of the MYP curriculum but that might be required by local authorities. While the courses provide students with a strong knowledge base, they emphasise the principles and concepts of the subject and approach topics from a variety of points of view, including the perspectives of other cultures.

MYP teachers use a variety of tools to assess student progress, including oral presentations, tests, essays and projects, and they apply the assessment criteria established by the IB to students' work. Schools may opt for official IB certification by asking the IB to validate their internal assessment. This is often referred to as the 'moderation system'. In this process, the IB reviews samples of the schools' assessment of student work and checks that schools are correctly applying the MYP assessment criteria. The IB offers guidance for teachers in the form of published examples of assessment.

The Primary Years Programme

The Primary Years Programme (PYP), for students aged 3 to 12, focuses on the development of the whole child, addressing social, physical, emotional and cultural needs. At the same time, it gives students a strong foundation in all the major areas of knowledge: mathematics, social studies, drama, language, music, visual arts, science, personal and social education, and physical education. The PYP aims to help students develop an international perspective – to become aware of and sensitive to the points of view of people in other parts of the world.

The PYP curriculum is organised around six themes:

- who we are;
- where we are in place and time;
- how we express ourselves;
- how the world works;
- how we organise ourselves;
- sharing the planet.

These themes are intended to help students make sense of themselves, of other people and of the physical environment, and to give them different ways of looking at the world. Assessment is used for two purposes: to guide teaching and to give students an opportunity to show, in a variety of ways, what they know and what they can do. In the PYP, assessment takes many forms. It ranges from completing checklists and monitoring progress to compiling a portfolio of a student's work. The IB offers schools substantial guidance for conducting assessment, including a detailed handbook and professional development workshops. Student portfolios and records of PYP exhibitions are reviewed on a regular basis by the IB as part of programme evaluation.

For further information about the IB programmes, please contact:

International Baccalaureate Programme
Route des Morillons 15
CH-1218 Grand-Saconnex
Geneva
Switzerland
Tel: + 41 22 791 7740
Fax: + 41 22 791 0277
E-mail: ibhq@ibo.org
Website: www.ibo.org

PART 1
SENIOR
SCHOOLS

300

THE GABBITAS TOP 300 INDEPENDENT SENIOR SCHOOLS

This section introduces the Top 300 senior schools. To begin with we explore the characteristics that place an independent school amongst the very best.

Successive governments in the UK have been rightly worried to see the country's ratings slip steadily down the international OECD/PISA league tables in the key subjects of reading (25th), maths (27th) and science (16th). While this has been the focus of much debate in politics and in the press, what is less often mentioned is the fact that, if you look at British independent schools on their own, their position is in the top three in every subject.

This does not mean, though, that only brilliant children go to independent schools. Indeed, one of the reasons for the sector's success is that it offers such a wide variety of schools. Parents can choose between boarding and day schools, single sex and co-ed, they can opt for schools in the cities or the countryside, or those that offer a particular speciality, such as music or drama, or a particular ethos, such as a faith school.

While such a variety may seem at first glance bewildering, what it does mean is that there will always be the right school to suit every child. The process will certainly begin with the child and most parents will know whether a very academic school will suit their child or whether they would be happier in an environment that focuses on their creativity. Moreover, parents can generally tell whether their child is likely to thrive in a boarding school with plenty of sport and activities or if they'd be more suited to one that was close to home and had a cosy, supportive ethos.

Academic success

One of the key factors everyone looks for from a school is, of course, good academic results – and independent schools here score highly and consistently. So what is the secret of their success? The majority start, of course, with a selective entry process. Winchester has an enviable reputation for academic success with regular results of more than 90 per cent of GCSEs at A or A*, over 75 per cent getting distinction at PreU and a large cohort going to Oxbridge. Director of Studies, James Webster explains, 'We pre-select at age 11 with tests in maths, English and IQ as well as an interview. Two years later, there is our entrance paper for academic scholarship and being a scholar carries quite a kudos – they're known here as the academic elite. We are a consciously academic school and that's all part of the ethos. We revel in learning.'

Dr Martin Stephen former High Master of St Paul's agrees: 'Once you have a reputation as a highly academic school, people who have clever children naturally gravitate towards you. But it's a reputation that is incredibly hard to acquire and all too easy to lose. And while you've got to have high quality pupils, you need equally high quality staff who are good at teaching very able children.'

Good teachers tend to recognise children's strengths and play to them. 'We have a great breadth of choice,' says Rodney Harris, Director of Studies at Westminster. 'You can do three sciences or, if you're a linguist you can do Latin, Greek, French and a second modern language. Our results speak for themselves.' (At Pre-U results are generally 65 per cent at the equivalent to A*, the best mark in the country, and in GCSEs over 95 per cent A* and A.)

Perhaps most importantly, in none of these schools will a hard-working or academic child be singled out as a 'geek'. Dr Jon Cox, headmaster of the Royal Grammar School, Guildford believes, 'Here it's cool to be bright. Our teachers take students off on tangents, get them fired up, encourage ideas, discussion and debating. Once you have a culture of scholarship, the boys spark off each other.'

Exam wars

Ultimately, all of this learning reaches the stage when it is tested in public examinations and while, as we have seen, independent schools have an outstanding record of success, there is also the question of which exam to take. In recent years, the A level has been challenged by two new exams: the Pre-U and the International Baccalaureate (IB), both offering a wider range of subjects to be taken by each student as well as, their supporters claim, a deeper challenge that helps universities decide between rival candidates. They have been partly in response to the considerable amount of hand wringing that has gone on during the last few years about the dumbing down of A

levels. However, the A* has effectively ended that debate with many universities demanding more than one A* for popular courses. Tony Little, Head of Eton, points out
when they were introduced there were 8 per cent of A*s. 'That's the same percentage
my generation got in As. So the A* is the new A.'

But what about the alternatives? At Haileybury, Master Joe Davies says, 'There has
been no grade inflation in IB over the last 20 years and I believe it's the best discrimin-
ator between the good, the very good and the best.' And it does, of course, have a
much broader range of subjects than the three or four most pupils take at A level. The
Pre-U is similar in this respect. Both, it is claimed, offer more 'stretch and challenge.'
Andrew Turner at Charterhouse believes, 'The Pre-U is certainly meatier and while it
requires more teaching time, we have the summer of the lower sixth that would otherwise be taken up with AS levels. And fewer exams means there's more time, too for all
the other things – sport, music, drama – that are getting squeezed out.'

More than exams

Aside from the exam successes that schools pride themselves on, one must consider
the other elements of school life that result in confident young adults ready for university
and the wider world. All good schools believe they should provide children with opportunities to be challenged, creative, physical, spiritual, even – gasp! – to have fun. This
makes sense on two levels. Firstly, it will create a happier, more confident child and,
secondly, a happier, more confident child will perform more successfully in every aspect of school life including those exams.

At Wellington College, Dr Anthony Seldon has created the Enrichment Octagon of
Opportunity with the aim of getting everyone to keep trying something new. Brynn
Bayman, Master in charge of Enrichment, explains, 'At the beginning of the school year
we have Carnival that works like Freshers' Week at university. There are jugglers, dancers,
candy floss and stalls for all the clubs selling their activities. It gets everyone thinking
out of the box and we encourage them to try something they wouldn't normally do –
rugby players knitting, academics dancing. It broadens their horizons.'

Clubs, societies and sport are all ways of building character, becoming a team
player and creating confidence – and independent schools encourage their students
to challenge themselves. In sport, the record is remarkable. In the Olympics, for
instance, 37 per cent of the Team GB winners were privately educated – though independent schools educate just 7 per cent of the population.

The extra-curricular choice is mind boggling. At City of London School for Girls they
have early morning zumba, at Gordonstoun they have skiing (including rollerski when
there's no snow in Scotland) and surfing. Dauntsey's have the *Jolie Brise* tall ship for
transatlantic racing, Winchester has book binding and illuminated manuscripts,

Ampleforth renovates old Land Rovers and has a pipe band, Bedales has stage fighting, a Middle East Society and a high-powered Maths Society. Eton has the Medical, Macmillan and Magical Societies (that's just the Ms) and St Edward's in Oxford has the Kenneth Grahame Society (an old boy) for some unnervingly radical interpretations of *The Wind in the Willows,* such as the role of the weasels in a socio-economic view as a threat to the Edwardian status quo.

Horses for courses

With such an extraordinary range of schools and activities on offer, how do you make the choice of which school will be right for which child? It really is a case of horses for courses – which school will bring out the strengths in which child. While some children will thrive in a very structured academic environment, others prefer a quite different approach. 'Some of the best lessons,' says Keith Budge, Head of Bedales, 'have a sense of discovery at their heart. We have an Outdoor Work department where pupils might take on a project like restoring an old tractor or building a barn. Not only does this generate massive enthusiasm, they learn about everything from wattle and daub to stress-bearing loads. We find the children love doing difficult things that test their ingenuity and curiosity.'

Joe Davies, Master at Haileybury, agrees: 'Teaching is no longer about standing at the front pontificating. There's group work, virtual learning, extended projects, role plays. The focus is on learning and that means finding out exactly how much *all* of the pupils have learned – not just the ones at the front. This reinforces the children's confidence.'

Sometimes, it's even a question of the school's location and history. 'I did an art history lesson,' says Stowe headmaster Anthony Wallersteiner, 'where I took them round bits of the mansion, particularly the Marble Hall [Stowe is blessed with the grandest of houses built by Robert Adam and Sir John Vanbrugh] where they drew the different kinds of capitals on the columns and I talked about the construction of the dome. Then we went into the North Hall where I got them to lie on the floor and look at the ceiling to identify the iconography and asked what it meant – they worked out that it was in victory you are generous to your foes. It's the same in science. Put a match into a test-tube of hydrogen and it goes bang – you'll remember that a lot more than someone just telling you.'

A school's location and history is important in other ways. 'Pupils here are aware,' says Ian Wilmshurst, Head of King's Bruton, 'that the history of their school goes back to 1519. We are proud of our heritage and ethos but the school constantly looks to develop and improve. Our A level results have been the best on record over the last three years. I believe that pupils will only fulfil their academic potential if they are well cared for and valued. Pastoral care is vital. A boarding school like ours thrives on the number of activities and opportunities on offer and the busier a pupil's life is the more successful they often are academically. The solo performance in the Summer Concert, the 50 runs on a Saturday afternoon, the prospect of completing Ten Tors all help to provide a sense of achievement. I recommend prospective parents judge us on our ethos and our sixth form pupils. The former cannot be quantified but it is virtually tangible, while the latter are young men and women who are employable, interesting, caring and, above all, confident without any trace of arrogance.'

At Lord Wandsworth they believe they produce confident young men and women, too: 'As a modest-sized school, we know each student and most staff live on campus so we have a village-like community. Teaching is also a real strength – teachers see being here as a way of life rather than merely a matter of teaching. So students who need additional support get plenty of study support and encouragement and one-to-one lessons are very common.'

This question of what is best for children who are not obviously academic is very important and this is where Value Added comes in – another independent school strength. In the simplest terms, it represents the difference between the grades a child is predicted to gain on joining and those actually achieved. Ian Lovat, Director of Studies at Ampleforth says, 'We take a wider range of ability than many of the bigger independent schools and certainly than the big day schools. We were recently placed in the top 3 per cent of schools for value added, reflecting the number of students who barely make the entry requirements for the sixth form and then go on to attain A level grades well beyond what might be expected. They are often classed as late developers.'

One of the highest achieving value added schools is Bede's in Eastbourne. 'The most important element in our success,' says Headmaster Dr Richard Maloney, 'is to have first class staff committed to excellence and the belief that every child can succeed. If the staff believe, the children will believe in themselves. Learning support is given as a normal part of school life – like doing film studies. And you always get everyone to aim for the top. If you tell them they'll succeed, they probably will.'

Much depends on the fine antennae of the staff. Sue Freestone, Head of King's School Ely says, 'The edge is we have smaller classes and pastoral systems that allow the teachers to know each child well. You know when they're working hard, if they're sparkling or gently dimming. They're nurtured but not mollycoddled. We encourage them to try things that make them grow in self-awareness and courage and this helps them cope with the pressure of exams. We are big celebrators here and achievement is recognised across the board – you find the passion and you reinforce it. It's all about self-belief.'

Passion can sometimes be so overwhelming it demands a certain choice of school. This is certainly true for many students attending Hurtwood House, the only Sixth Form boarding school in the country with creativity and performance at its core. 'Technically,' says Headmaster Richard Jackson, 'they're good enough to go straight on to television and when the students leave they can show a portfolio or a showreel and say 'Look, I'm employable. I understand every principle about this.' They have a film studio with a new edit suite, recording studios and the latest professional technology for music, film, photography and theatre. 'When we do a school play,' says Jackson, 'we have a West End orchestra for 12 nights. By the time you leave here you're already at the same level as the second year in a drama school.' But it's not all about putting on a show. At the same time as producing alumni like Emily Blunt, they send seven or eight people a year to Oxbridge and they have one of the top value added ratings in the country.

At Tring Park School for the Performing Arts, too, they manage to balance vocational training with excellent academic results. Principal Stefan Anderson says, 'We have a day that's half academic, half vocational. You know the old adage – if you want something done, give it to a busy person. Here the students have four or five hours of dance or music or drama every day. They have to learn to manage time really well and everyone gives 110 per cent.'

An education for all?

While independent schools educate only a minority of the UK population, that does not mean the door is closed on financial grounds to anyone who aspires to go to one of them. At many schools there are not only scholarships that are linked to excellence (academic, musical, sport) but also growing numbers of bursaries. At schools like Harrow, for instance, a child will compete for a scholarship 'means blind' and if successful will be given a bursary according to his needs – there are 60 a year ranging from 5–100 per cent of the fees. Charterhouse also offers bursaries for those who need them to top up their scholarships to 100 per cent of the fees – and in one case even paid half of the prep fees before a pupil joined at 13.

The biggest and most long established public schools, such as Rugby and Eton, can find the money most easily as they tend to have the biggest foundation funds but virtually all independent schools are putting some money into bursaries nowadays rather than scholarships because they see this as the fairest way forward. Schools such as Ampleforth, St Edward's in Oxford and St Paul's Girls still have scholarships but the financial reward is largely honorary and there are bursaries for those who need them. Some schools have set up innovative systems – Brighton College for instance has an arrangement with Kingsford Community School in Newham, East London giving three or four full boarding scholarships a year for pupils to join their sixth form. Gordonstoun, one of the original test cases for the Charity Commission, had 80 pupils with means-tested support so passed its test with flying colours.

Often a prep school that has links with the senior school will suggest a pupil for a scholarship or bursary. However, the schools are always glad to hear from parents who would like to discuss the possibilities.

A firm foundation

There is little doubt that independent schools offer their students an outstanding education as well as great preparation for university and beyond. It is that mysterious combination of academic success, personal challenges, broad extra-curricular activities, strong pastoral care and a school ethos that has developed in many cases over centuries. The result is an education widely regarded as the best in the world.

> *"Thank you so much — what a transformation. I now have a boy who is like an exocet missile — totally focussed and determined to succeed — I simply can't thank you enough."*
>
> **Cathy Hutton, Hampshire**

Photo: Blundell's

Tailor made services for parents

▸ Schools placement advice for parents interested in day, boarding, prep and senior school

▸ Hourly tuition in all subjects, at all stages: from Key Stage 1 to degree level

☎ **+44 (0)20 7734 0161**

@ **schools@gabbitas.co.uk**

⊕ **www.gabbitas.co.uk**

SENIOR SCHOOLS
LISTING

P = Also in Profiled Schools section

NB   Age ranges are shown for the senior school only.
      Age ranges for prep and/or pre-prep departments are not included.

Abbey Gate College, Cheshire **P**
Co-ed, Day only, 11–18

The Abbey School, Berkshire **P**
Girls, Day only, 11–18

Abingdon School, Oxfordshire
Boys, Day and Boarding, 11–18

Aldenham School, Hertfordshire
Co-ed, Boarding and Day, 11–18

Alleyn's School, London
Co-ed, Day only, 11–18

Ampleforth College, North Yorkshire
Co-ed, Boarding and Day, 13–18

Ardingly College, West Sussex
Co-ed, Boarding and Day, 11–17

Arnold School, Lancashire
Co-ed, Day only, 11–18

Ashford School, Kent
Co-ed, Day and Boarding, 11–18

Bablake School, West Midlands
Co-ed, Day only, 11–19

Badminton School, Bristol **P**
Girls, Boarding and Day, 11–18

Bancroft's School, Essex **P**
Co-ed, Day only, 11–18

Bedales School, Hampshire
Co-ed, Boarding and Day, 13–18

Bede's, East Sussex
Co-ed, Boarding and Day, 13–19

Bedford Girls School, Bedfordshire
Girls, Day and Boarding, 11–18

Bedford Modern School,
Bedfordshire
Co-ed, Day only, 11–18

Bedford School, Bedfordshire **P**
Boys, Day and Boarding, 13–18

Benenden School, Kent
Girls, Boarding only, 11–18

Berkhamsted School, Hertfordshire
Co-ed, Day and Boarding, 11–18

Birkdale School, South Yorkshire
Boys, Day only, 11–18

Birkenhead School, Merseyside
Co-ed, Day only, 11–18

Bishop's Stortford College,
Hertfordshire
Co-ed, Day and Boarding, 13–18

Blundell's School, Devon **P**
Co-ed, Boarding and Day, 11–18

Bolton School (Boys' Division),
Lancashire
Boys, Day only, 13–18

Bolton School (Girls' Division),
Lancashire
Girls, Day only, 11–18

Bootham School, North Yorkshire
Co-ed, Boarding and Day, 11–18

Box Hill School, Surrey
Co-ed, Boarding and Day, 11–18

Bradfield College, Berkshire **P**
Co-ed, Boarding and Day, 13–18

Bradford Grammar School, West
Yorkshire
Co-ed, Day only, 11–18

Brentwood School, Essex
Co-ed, Day and Boarding, 11–18

**Brighton and Hove High School
GDST**, East Sussex
Girls, Day only, 11–18

Brighton College, East Sussex
Co-ed, Day and Boarding, 11–18

Bristol Grammar School, Bristol **P**
Co-ed, Day only, 11–18

Bromsgrove School, **P**
Worcestershire
Co-ed, Boarding and Day, 13–18

Bruton School for Girls, **P**
Somerset
Girls, Day and Boarding, 11–18

Bryanston School, Dorset **P**
Co-ed, Boarding and Day, 13–18

Bury Grammar School Boys,
Lancashire
Boys, Day only, 11–18

Bury Grammar School Girls,
Lancashire
Girls, Day only, 11–18

Campbell College, County Antrim,
Northern Ireland
Boys, Boarding and Day, 11–18

Canford School, Dorset **P**
Co-ed, Boarding and Day, 13–18

Caterham School, Surrey
Co-ed, Day and Boarding, 11–18

Charterhouse, Surrey ⓟ
Boys, Boarding and Day, 13–18

Chase Academy, Staffordshire
Co-ed, Day and Boarding, 11–18

Cheadle Hulme School, Cheshire
Co-ed, Day only, 11–18

Cheltenham College, Gloucestershire
Co-ed, Boarding and Day, 13–18

Cheltenham Ladies' College,
Gloucestershire
Girls, Boarding and Day, 11–18

Chetham's School of Music, Greater
Manchester
Co-ed, Boarding and Day, 11–18

Chigwell School, Essex
Co-ed, Day and Boarding, 11–18

Christ College, Powys, Wales
Co-ed, Boarding and Day, 11–18

Christ's Hospital, West Sussex ⓟ
Co-ed, Boarding and Day, 11–18

Churchers College Senior School,
Hampshire
Co-ed, Day only, 11–18

City of London Freemen's School,
Surrey
Co-ed, Day and Boarding, 11–18

City of London School for Girls,
London
Girls, Day only, 11–18

City of London School, London ⓟ
Boys, Day only, 10–18

Claremont Fan Court School,
Surrey
Co-ed, Day only, 11–18

Clayesmore, Dorset ⓟ
Co-ed, Boarding and Day, 13–18

Clifton College, Bristol ⓟ
Co-ed, Boarding and Day, 13–18

Clifton High School, Bristol
Co-ed, Day and Boarding, 11–18

Cobham Hall, Kent ⓟ
Girls, Boarding and Day, 11–18

Colfe's School, London
Co-ed, Day only, 11–18

Cranleigh School, Surrey
Co-ed, Boarding and Day, 13–18

Culford School, Suffolk ⓟ
Co-ed, Boarding and Day, 13–18

d'Overbroeck's College Oxford,
Oxfordshire
Co-ed, Day and Boarding, 11–19

Dame Allan's Boys School, Tyne and
Wear
Boys, Day only, 13–18

Dame Allan's Girls School, Tyne and
Wear
Girls, Day only, 11–18

Dauntsey's School, Wiltshire **P**
Co-ed, Boarding and Day, 11–18

Dean Close School, Gloucestershire
Co-ed, Boarding and Day, 13–18

Derby Grammar School, Derbyshire
Co-ed, Day only, 11–18

Derby High School, Derbyshire
Co-ed, Day only, 11–18

Dollar Academy, Clackmannanshire
Co-ed, Day and Boarding, 11–18

Downe House, Berkshire
Girls, Boarding and Day, 11–18

Downside School, Somerset **P**
Co-ed, Boarding and Day, 13–18

Dulwich College, London
Boys, Day and Boarding, 13–18

Durham High School for Girls,
County Durham
Girls, Day only, 11–18

Eastbourne College, East Sussex **P**
Co-ed, Boarding and Day, 13–18

Edgbaston High School for Girls,
West Midlands **P**
Girls, Day only, 11–18

The Edinburgh Academy, Lothian
Boys, Day and Boarding, 13–18

Elizabeth College, Channel Islands
Co-ed, Day only, 11–18

Eltham College, London
Boys, Day only, 13–18

Epsom College, Surrey **P**
Co-ed, Boarding and Day, 13–18

Eton College, Berkshire
Boys, Boarding only, 13–18

Exeter School, Devon
Co-ed, Day only, 11–18

Felsted School, Essex
Co-ed, Boarding and Day, 13–18

Fettes College, Lothian
Co-ed, Boarding and Day, 11–18

Forest School, London **P**
Co-ed, Day only, 11–18

Framlingham College, Suffolk **P**
Co-ed, Boarding and Day, 13–18

**Francis Holland School, Regent's
Park NW1**, London **P**
Girls, Day only, 11–18

Frensham Heights School, **P**
Surrey
Co-ed, Day and Boarding, 11–18

George Heriot's School, Lothian
Co-ed, Day only, 11–18

George Watson's College, Lothian
Co-ed, Day only, 11–18

Giggleswick School, North Yorkshire
Co-ed, Boarding and Day, 11–18

The Glasgow Academy, Glasgow
Co-ed, Day only, 11–18

Glenalmond College,
Perth and Kinross **℗**
Co-ed, Boarding and Day, 12–18

The Godolphin and Latymer School,
London
Girls, Day only, 11–18

The Godolphin School, Wiltshire
Girls, Boarding and Day, 11–18

Gordonstoun School, Morayshire **℗**
Co-ed, Boarding and Day, 8–18

The Grammar School at Leeds, West
Yorkshire
Co-ed, Day only, 11–18

The Grange School, Cheshire
Co-ed, Day only, 11–18

Gresham's School, Norfolk
Co-ed, Boarding and Day, 13–18

Guildford High School, Surrey
Girls, Day only, 11–18

Haberdashers' Aske's Boys' School,
Hertfordshire
Boys, Day only, 11–18

**Haberdashers' Aske's School for
Girls,** Hertfordshire
Girls, Day only, 11–18

**Haberdashers' Monmouth School
For Girls,** Monmouthshire, Wales
Girls, Day and Boarding, 11–18

Haileybury, Hertfordshire **℗**
Co-ed, Boarding and Day, 11–18

Hampton School, Middlesex **℗**
Boys, Day only, 11–18

Harrogate Ladies' College, North
Yorkshire **℗**
Girls, Boarding and Day, 11–18

Harrow School, Middlesex
Boys, Boarding only, 13–18

Headington School, Oxfordshire
Girls, Day and Boarding, 11–18

Heathfield School, Ascot **℗**
Girls, Boarding only, 11–18

Heathfield School for Girls,
Middlesex **℗**
Girls, Day only, 11–18

Hereford Cathedral School,
Herefordshire
Co-ed, Day only, 11–18

Highgate School, London
Co-ed, Day only, 11–18

Hurstpierpoint College, West Sussex
Co-ed, Boarding and Day, 11–18

Hurtwood House, Surrey **ⓟ**
Co-ed, Boarding and Day, 16–18

Hymers College, East Riding of
Yorkshire
Co-ed, Day only, 11–18

Immanuel College, Hertfordshire
Co-ed, Day only, 11–18

Ipswich School, Suffolk
Co-ed, Day and Boarding, 11–18

James Allen's Girls' School, London
Girls, Day only, 11–18

The John Lyon School, Middlesex
Boys, Day only, 11–18

Kelly College, Devon **ⓟ**
Co-ed, Day and Boarding, 11–18

Kent College Canterbury, Kent **ⓟ**
Co-ed, Day and Boarding, 11–18

Kent College Pembury, Kent
Girls, Boarding and Day, 11–18

Kilgraston, Perth and Kinross
Girls, Boarding and Day, 11–18

Kimbolton School, Cambridgeshire
Co-ed, Boarding and Day, 11–18

**King Edward VI High School for
Girls,** West Midlands
Girls, Day only, 11–18

King Edward VI School, Hampshire
Co-ed, Day only, 11–18

King Edward's School, Bath, Bath &
North East Somerset **ⓟ**
Co-ed, Day only, 11–18

King Edward's School, West Midlands
Boys, Day only, 11–18

King Henry VIII School, West
Midlands **ⓟ**
Co-ed, Day only, 11–18

King's Bruton, Somerset **ⓟ**
Co-ed, Boarding and Day, 13–18

King's College School, London
Boys, Day only, 13–18

King's College, Somerset
Co-ed, Boarding and Day, 13–18

King's Ely, **ⓟ**
Cambridgeshire
Co-ed, Day and Boarding, 13–18

King's Rochester, Kent
Co-ed, Day and Boarding, 11–18

The King's School, Worcestershire
Co-ed, Day only, 11–18

The King's School, Gloucestershire
Co-ed, Day only, 11–18

The King's School, Kent
Co-ed, Boarding and Day, 13–18

The King's School, Cheshire
Co-ed, Day only, 11–18

The King's School, Cheshire
Co-ed, Day only, 11–18

Kingston Grammar School, Surrey
Co-ed, Day only, 11–18

Kingswood School, Bath & North East
Somerset **P**
Co-ed, Boarding and Day, 11–18

Kirkham Grammar School,
Lancashire
Co-ed, Boarding and Day, 11–18

The Lady Eleanor Holles School,
Middlesex
Girls, Day only, 11–18

Lancing College, West Sussex **P**
Co-ed, Boarding and Day, 13–18

Latymer Upper School, London
Co-ed, Day only, 11–18

Leicester Grammar School,
Leicestershire
Co-ed, Day only, 11–18

Leicester High School For Girls,
Leicestershire
Girls, Day only, 11–18

Leighton Park School, Berkshire **P**
Co-ed, Boarding and Day, 11–18

The Leys School, **P**
Cambridgeshire
Co-ed, Boarding and Day, 11–18

Lichfield Cathedral School,
Staffordshire **P**
Co-ed, Day and Boarding, 11–18

Lincoln Minster School, Lincolnshire
Co-ed, Day and Boarding, 11–18

Llandovery College, Carmarthenshire,
Wales **P**
Co-ed, Boarding and Day, 11–18

Lord Wandsworth College,
Hampshire **P**
Co-ed, Boarding and Day, 11–18

Loughborough Grammar School,
Leicestershire
Boys, Day and Boarding, 13–18

LVS Ascot, Berkshire
Co-ed, Boarding and Day, 11–18

Magdalen College School,
Oxfordshire
Co-ed, Day only, 11–18

Malvern College, Worcestershire
Co-ed, Boarding and Day, 13–18

Malvern St James Girls' School,
Worcestershire **P**
Girls, Boarding and Day, 11–18

The Manchester Grammar School,
Greater Manchester
Boys, Day only, 11–18

Manchester High School for Girls,
Greater Manchester
Girls, Day only, 11–18

Marlborough College, Wiltshire
Co-ed, Boarding and Day, 13–18

The Mary Erskine School, Lothian
Girls, Day and Boarding, 12–18

The Maynard School, Devon
Girls, Day only, 11–18

Merchant Taylors' Boys' Schools,
Merseyside
Boys, Day only, 13–18

Merchant Taylors' Girls' School,
Merseyside
Girls, Day only, 11–18

Merchant Taylors' School, Middlesex
Boys, Day only, 11–18

Merchiston Castle School,
Lothian
Boys, Boarding and Day, 13–18

Methodist College, County Antrim
Co-ed, Day and Boarding, 11–19

Mill Hill School, London
Co-ed, Boarding and Day, 13–18

Millfield School, Somerset
Co-ed, Boarding and Day, 13–18

Monkton Senior School, Bath & North
East Somerset
Co-ed, Boarding and Day, 11–19

Monmouth School, Monmouthshire,
Wales
Boys, Boarding and Day, 13–18

Moreton Hall School, Shropshire
Girls, Boarding and Day, 11–18

Morrison's Academy, Perth and
Kinross
Co-ed, Day only, 11–18

New Hall School, Essex
Co-ed, Boarding and Day, 11–18

Newcastle-under-Lyme School,
Staffordshire
Co-ed, Day only, 11–18

North London Collegiate, Middlesex
Girls, Day only, 11–18

**Norwich High School for Girls
GDST**, Norfolk
Girls, Day only, 11–18

Norwich School, Norfolk
Co-ed, Day only, 11–18

**Nottingham High School for Girls
GDST**, Nottinghamshire
Girls, Day only, 11–18

Nottingham High School,
Nottinghamshire
Boys, Day only, 11–18

Oakham School, Rutland **P**
Co-ed, Boarding and Day, 13–18

Old Palace of John Whitgift School,
Surrey **P**
Girls, Day only, 10–18

The Oratory School, Berkshire
Boys, Day and Boarding, 11–18

Oundle School, Northamptonshire
Co-ed, Boarding and Day, 11–19

Our Lady's Abingdon School,
Oxfordshire **P**
Co-ed, Day only, 11–18

Oxford High School GDST,
Oxfordshire
Girls, Day only, 11–18

Padworth College, Berkshire
Co-ed, Boarding and Day, 13–19

Pangbourne College, Berkshire
Co-ed, Boarding and Day, 11–18

The Perse School, Cambridgeshire
Co-ed, Day only, 11–18

Plymouth College, Devon
Co-ed, Day and Boarding, 11–18

Pocklington School, East Riding of
Yorkshire
Co-ed, Boarding and Day, 11–18

The Portsmouth Grammar School,
Hampshire
Co-ed, Day only, 11–18

Prior Park College, Bath & North East
Somerset **P**
Co-ed, Boarding and Day, 13–18

Prior's Field, Surrey **P**
Girls, Day and Boarding, 11–18

The Purcell School, Hertfordshire
Co-ed, Day and Boarding, 11–18

Putney High School GDST, London
Girls, Day only, 11–18

Queen Anne's School, Berkshire
Girls, Boarding and Day, 11–18

Queen Elizabeth Grammar School,
West Yorkshire
Boys, Day only, 13–18

Queen Elizabeth's Grammar School,
Lancashire
Co-ed, Day only, 11–18

Queen Elizabeth's Hospital, Bristol
Boys, Day only, 13–18

Queen's College, Somerset
Co-ed, Day and Boarding, 11–18

The Queen's School, Cheshire
Girls, Day only, 11–18

Queenswood, Hertfordshire
Girls, Boarding and Day, 11–18

Radley College, Oxfordshire
Boys, Boarding only, 13–18

Reading Blue Coat School, **P**
Berkshire
Boys, Day only, 11–18

The Red Maids' School, Bristol
Girls, Day only, 11–18

Redland High School for Girls,
Bristol
Girls, Day only, 11–18

Reed's School, Surrey
Boys, Boarding and Day, 11–18

Reigate Grammar School, Surrey
Co-ed, Day only, 11–18

Rendcomb College, Gloucestershire
Co-ed, Day and Boarding, 11–18

Repton School, Derbyshire
Co-ed, Boarding and Day, 13–18

RGS Worcester & The Alice Ottley
School, Worcestershire
Co-ed, Day only, 11–18

Robert Gordon's College,
Aberdeenshire
Co-ed, Day only, 11–18

Roedean School, East Sussex
Girls, Boarding and Day, 11–18

Rossall School, Lancashire
Co-ed, Day and Boarding, 11–18

Royal Grammar School, Guildford,
Surrey **P**
Boys, Day only, 11–18

Royal Grammar School, Tyne and
Wear
Boys, Day only, 8–18

The Royal High School, Bath, Bath &
North East Somerset **P**
Girls, Day and Boarding, 11–18

The Royal Hospital School, **P**
Suffolk
Co-ed, Boarding and Day, 11–18

The Royal Masonic School for Girls,
Hertfordshire **P**
Girls, Day and Boarding, 11–18

Royal Russell School, Surrey
Co-ed, Boarding and Day, 11–18

Rugby School, Warwickshire
Co-ed, Boarding and Day, 11–18

Rydal Penrhos School, Conwy, Wales
Co-ed, Boarding and Day, 11–18

Ryde School, Isle of Wight
Co-ed, Day and Boarding, 11–18

Seaford College, West Sussex **ⓟ**
Co-ed, Day and Boarding, 13–18

Sedbergh School, Cumbria
Co-ed, Boarding and Day, 13–18

Sevenoaks School, Kent
Co-ed, Day and Boarding, 11–18

Sheffield High School GDST, South
Yorkshire
Girls, Day only, 11–18

Sherborne Girls, Dorset
Girls, Boarding and Day, 11–18

Shiplake College, Oxfordshire
Co-ed, Day and Boarding, 11–18

Shrewsbury High School GDST,
Shropshire
Co-ed, Day only, 11–18

Shrewsbury School, Shropshire
Co-ed, Boarding and Day, 13–18

Sibford School, Oxfordshire
Co-ed, Boarding and Day, 11–18

Silcoates School, West Yorkshire
Co-ed, Day only, 11–18

Sir William Perkins's School, Surrey
Girls, Day only, 11–18

Solihull School, West Midlands
Co-ed, Day only, 11–18

South Hampstead High School,
London
Girls, Day only, 11–18

St Albans School, Hertfordshire **ⓟ**
Boys, Day only, 11–18

St Bede's College, Greater
Manchester
Co-ed, Day only, 11–18

St Bees School, Cumbria
Co-ed, Boarding and Day, 11–18

St Benedict's School, London **ⓟ**
Co-ed, Day only, 11–18

St Columba's College, Hertfordshire
Boys, Day only, 11–18

St Dunstan's College, London
Co-ed, Day only, 11–18

St Edmund's College, **ⓟ**
Hertfordshire
Co-ed, Day and Boarding, 11–18

St Edmund's School Canterbury,
Kent
Co-ed, Day and Boarding, 11–18

St Edward's School, Oxfordshire **ⓟ**
Co-ed, Boarding and Day, 13–18

St George's College, Surrey
Co-ed, Day only, 11–18

St Helen & St Katharine, **P**
Oxfordshire
Girls, Day only, 11–18

St James Independent School for Boys (Senior), Surrey
Boys, Day and Boarding, 10–18

St John's School, Surrey
Co-ed, Boarding and Day, 13–18

St Leonards School, Fife
Co-ed, Boarding and Day, 11–19

St Leonards-Mayfield School, **P**
East Sussex
Girls, Day and Boarding, 11–18

St Mary's Calne, Wiltshire
Girls, Boarding and Day, 11–18

St Mary's School, Ascot, **P**
Berkshire
Girls, Boarding and Day, 11–18

St Mary's School, Shaftesbury, **P**
Dorset
Girls, Boarding and Day, 11–18

St Paul's Girls' School, London
Girls, Day only, 11–18

St Paul's School, London
Boys, Day and Boarding, 13–18

St Peter's School, North Yorkshire
Co-ed, Boarding and Day, 11–18

Stamford High School, Lincolnshire
Girls, Day and Boarding, 11–18

Stamford School, Lincolnshire
Boys, Day and Boarding, 11–18

Stewart's Melville College, Lothian
Boys, Day and Boarding, 12–18

Stockport Grammar School, Cheshire
Co-ed, Day only, 11–18

Stonyhurst College, Lancashire **P**
Co-ed, Boarding and Day, 13–18

Stowe School, Buckinghamshire
Co-ed, Boarding and Day, 13–18

Strathallan School, Perthshire **P**
Co-ed, Boarding and Day, 13–18

Surbiton High School, Surrey **P**
Girls, Day only, 11–18

Sutton High School GDST, Surrey
Girls, Day only, 11–18

Sutton Valence School, Kent
Co-ed, Boarding and Day, 11–18

Taunton School Senior, Somerset
Co-ed, Boarding and Day, 13–18

Thetford Grammar School, **P**
Norfolk
Co-ed, Day only, 11–18

Tonbridge School, Kent
Boys, Boarding and Day, 13–18

Tormead School, Surrey **P**
Girls, Day only, 11–18

**Tring Park School for the
Performing Arts**, Hertfordshire **P**
Co-ed, Boarding and Day, 11–19

Trinity School, Surrey
Boys, Day only, 13–18

Truro School, Cornwall
Co-ed, Day and Boarding, 11–18

Tudor Hall School, Oxfordshire **P**
Girls, Boarding and Day, 11–18

University College School, London
Co-ed, Day only, 11–18

Uppingham School, Rutland **P**
Co-ed, Boarding and Day, 13–18

Victoria College, Channel Islands
Boys, Day only, 11–19

Wakefield Girls' High School,
West Yorkshire
Girls, Day only, 11–18

Warminster School, Wiltshire
Co-ed, Boarding and Day, 11–19

Warwick School, Warwickshire
Boys, Day and Boarding, 13–18

Wellington College, Berkshire **P**
Co-ed, Boarding and Day, 13–18

Wellington School, Somerset
Co-ed, Boarding and Day, 11–18

Wells Cathedral School, Somerset
Co-ed, Boarding and Day, 11–18

Westminster, London **P**
Co-ed, Boarding and Day, 13–18

Whitgift School, Surrey **P**
Boys, Day only, 11–18

Wimbledon High School GDST,
London
Girls, Day only, 11–18

Winchester College, Hampshire
Boys, Boarding and Day, 13–18

Wisbech Grammar School,
Cambridgeshire
Co-ed, Day only, 11–18

Withington Girls' School,
Greater Manchester **P**
Girls, Day only, 11–18

Woldingham School, Surrey
Girls, Boarding and Day, 11–18

Wolverhampton Grammar School,
West Midlands
Co-ed, Day only, 11–18

Woodhouse Grove School, West
Yorkshire
Co-ed, Boarding and Day, 11–18

Worksop College, Nottinghamshire
Co-ed, Boarding and Day, 13–18

Worth School, West Sussex
Co-ed, Boarding and Day, 11–18

Wycliffe College, Gloucestershire
Co-ed, Boarding and Day, 11–18

Wycombe Abbey School,
Buckinghamshire
Girls, Boarding and Day, 11–18

Yarm School, Stockton-on-Tees
Co-ed, Day only, 11–18

SENIOR SCHOOLS
PROFILED SCHOOLS

Notes on the Senior Schools Profiled Schools

Age ranges in the shaded details box are for the senior school only. Age ranges for any preparatory and/or pre-preparatory departments aren't included, although they may be mentioned in the text. Only memberships relating to the senior school are included. For more details on memberships please see the glossary that appears towards the end of the book.

Abbey Gate College, Cheshire, England

Co-ed, Day only, 11–18

Head Mrs T Pollard
Saighton Grange, Saighton Lane
Saighton
Chester
Cheshire
England
CH3 6EN
T: 01244 332077
E: bursar@abbeygatecollege.co.uk
W: www.abbeygatecollege.co.uk

Age range 11–18
No of pupils 511; Girls 231; Boys 280
Religious denomination
  Inter-Denominational
Founded 1977
Member of AGBIS, ISA, ISBA, SHMIS
Fees £7,440–£10,875

Abbey Gate College is a well-established, coeducational school for pupils aged 4–18. The college emphasises the importance of building a love of learning in a caring and nurturing environment. Examination results are strong and the extra curricular programme provides many opportunities for our pupils. The College is a successful and happy school, committed to maintaining traditional standards and high educational ideals. The latest inspection recognised that, 'Students achieve their academic and personal potential', whilst also commending the 'high standards of teaching, learning and especially behaviour in the college'. We invite you to make an appointment to come and tour our fantastic grounds and facilities and let our pupils tell you why Abbey Gate College provides them with a first class education.

The Abbey School, Berkshire, England

Girls, Day only, 11–18

The Abbey School

Head Mistress Mrs B E Stanley
17 Kendrick Road
Reading
Berkshire
England
RG1 5DZ
T: 0118 987 2256
E: admissions@theabbey.co.uk
W: www.theabbey.co.uk

Age range 11–18
No of pupils 1091; Girls 1091
Religious denomination Christian
Founded 1887
Member of AGBIS, GSA, IB, ISA, ISBA
Fees £8,790–£13,980

The Abbey School is a warm and welcoming community of 1100 girls aged 3–18. The school offers an outstanding academic programme supported by strong pastoral care and an exceptional range of extra-curricular opportunities. Girls are encouraged to discover their talents and passions and to develop the leadership and team-working skills that will equip them to lead happy and fulfilling lives. Students at The Abbey excel academically, with 61% of A level and 83% of GCSE papers graded at A*/A in 2012. Our IB Diploma students achieved an average score of 39 points in 2013. The rich variety of opportunities for sport, art, drama, and music ensure that the school is a busy and exciting place, where a strong community spirit and boundless enthusiasm from students and staff create a wonderful learning environment.

Badminton School, Bristol, England

Girls, Boarding and Day, 11–18

Badminton School
Bristol

The Headmistress Mrs R Tear
Westbury Road, Westbury-on-Trym
Bristol
England
BS9 3BA
T: 0117 905 5271
E: admissions@badminton.bristol.sch.uk
W: www.badminton.bristol.sch.uk

Age range 11–18
No of pupils 450; Girls 450
Religious denomination
   Non-Denominational
Founded 1858
Member of AGBIS, BSA, GSA, ISBA
Fees £15,510–£30,840

Badminton is a thriving day and boarding school for girls, which has remained at the forefront of girls' education for well over 150 years. We are enormously proud of our heritage and traditions, but are certainly not constrained by them. The size of the campus and community gives a homely and vibrant feel to the School. This, coupled with our excellent pastoral care, leaves no scope for anonymity, but rather lends itself to strong mutually supportive relationships between girls as well as between girls and staff. Whilst the school retains a nationally outstanding academic record, its focus continues to be on nurturing the girls' natural curiosity and fuelling their passion for learning. Therefore, we select girls on their personal strengths and all round ability, as well as their academic potential. It is a characteristic of Badminton girls that they are thoughtful individuals, able to evaluate information and decide for themselves. This approach extends beyond their studies and into the day to day life of the School, where girls are given a wide range of opportunities to grow, develop and express themselves in an enormous range of activities.

Bancroft's School, Essex, England

Co-ed, Day only, 11–18

Head Mrs M E Ireland
High Road
Woodford Green
Essex
England
IG10 4NX
T: 020 8505 4821
E: office@bancrofts.org
W: www.bancrofts.org

Age range 11–18
No of pupils 840; Girls 385; Boys 455
Religious denomination Church of
England
Founded 1737
Member of HMC
Fees £14,130

Bancroft's is a dynamic, cosmopolitan environment in which bright children are stimulated and inspired to achieve in all areas of their school careers. Pupils here are eager to learn and to be successful and the School is renowned for academic excellence. Bancroftians achieve consistently high standards in public examinations. Enthusiastic and committed teachers display not only a passion for their subjects but also a passion for inspiring pupils to do their best. An exciting programme of sporting and co-curricular opportunities contributes to the School's vibrancy, encouraging pupils to discover talents and passions beyond the classroom. This varied and stimulating choice of activities, everything from chess and craft to the CCF, means that there really is something to suit everyone.

Bedford School, Bedfordshire, England

Boys, Day and Boarding, 13–18

Head Master Mr J S Moule	**Age range** 13–18
De Parys Avenue	**No of pupils** 1109; Boys 1109
Bedford	**Religious denomination**
Bedfordshire	Church of England
England	**Founded** 1552
MK40 2TU	**Member of** HMC, IB
T: 01234 362216	**Fees** £10,806–£28,200
E: admissions@bedfordschool.org.uk	
W: www.bedfordschool.org.uk	

Bedford School is an independent boarding and day school that offers boys aged 7–18 (seniors from 13) a complete and balanced education; that teaches pupils to think intelligently, act wisely and be fully engaged in a challenging and changing world. Academic ambition is strongly encouraged and supported throughout the school, and pupils enjoy demanding lessons that are designed to challenge intellectually and to inspire natural curiosity. The school is also renowned for its strengths in music, the arts and sport. Outside the classroom, boys enjoy an outstanding variety of extracurricular activities intended to foster independence and community spirit among pupils of all ages. Set in a beautiful and extensive estate in the heart of Bedford, the school is just 50 miles north of London and within easy reach of Heathrow Airport.

Blundell's School, Devon, England

Co-ed, Boarding and Day, 11–18

Head Mrs N Huggett
Blundells Road
Tiverton
Devon
England
EX16 4DN
T: 01884 252543
E: info@blundells.org
W: www.blundells.org

Age range 11–18
No of pupils 567; Girls 225; Boys 342
Religious denomination Church of
England
Founded 1604
Member of BSA, HMC
Fees £14,550–£28,200

Blundell's is an independent school for full, weekly and flexi boarding and day pupils. It combines strong academic achievement and excellent facilities with the best pastoral care: the welfare and happiness of our pupils are top priorities. The strength of Blundell's School lies in the diversity of options which gives every pupil a chance to shine. Blundell's also has a richly deserved reputation for sport, drama, music and art. The deep and enduring friendships formed at Blundell's, fostered by the school's fantastic community spirit, together with the intellectual, physical and cultural interests they develop here, provide our pupils with skills for life. Blundell's has an adjoining day prep school for ages 3–11 and is easily accessible by road, rail and air.

Bradfield College, Berkshire, England

Co-ed, Boarding and Day, 13–18

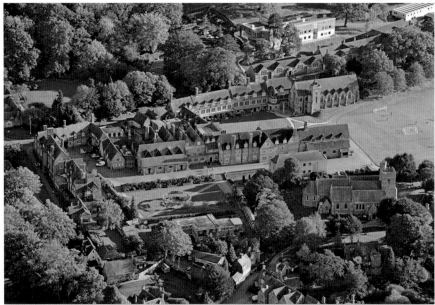

Head Mr S C Henderson
Bradfield
Reading
Berkshire
England
RG7 6AU
T: 0118 964 4516
E: admissions@bradfieldcollege.org.uk
W: www.bradfieldcollege.org.uk

Age range 13–18; Entry at 13+ (Year 9)
and Sixth Form
No of pupils 730; Girls 256; Boys 474
Religious denomination Church of
England
Founded 1850
Member of BSA, HMC, IB
Fees £25,752–£32,190

Bradfield College, set in beautiful Berkshire countryside, delivers an outstanding academic education for all, unparalleled pastoral care and a diverse range of co-curricular activities, enabling every individual to find his or her niche. The College offers a wide selection of subjects in both the Junior and Senior schools, including the IB at Sixth Form, providing challenge and choice through personalised programmes of study, inspired by passionate and engaging teaching. Academic Scholarships and Dr Gray All-Rounder Exhibitions are available at 13+ and 16+, as are means-tested Bursaries. Entrance to the large and vibrant Sixth Form is conditional on attainment of a minimum of 6 B grades at GCSE, assessment at Bradfield and Headteacher's reference.

Bristol Grammar School,

Bristol, England

Co-ed, Day only, 11–18

Bristol
Grammar
School

Head Master Mr R I MacKinnon
University Road
Bristol
England
BS8 1SR
T: 0117 973 6006
E: website@bgs.bristol.sch.uk
W: www.bristolgrammarschool.co.uk

Age range 11–18
No of pupils 960; Girls 480; Boys 480
Religious denomination
Non-Denominational
Founded 1532
Member of HMC, SHMIS
Fees £6,825–£12,840

Bristol Grammar School aims high and is proud to do so, inspiring a love of learning, self-confidence and a sense of adventure among its pupils. Founded almost 500 years ago, BGS is an independent co-educational day school for pupils aged 4 to 18 and considered one of the leading academic schools in the South West. BGS provides an excellent education, developing independence of thought through high-quality teaching of a broad curriculum and wide-ranging intellectual, physical and cultural pursuits. An exceptional pastoral care system, based around six Houses, gives every pupil a sense of belonging and the security and confidence to make the most of the opportunities offered. Prospective pupils and their families are most welcome to visit, with tours available throughout the year.

Bromsgrove School, Worcestershire, England

Co-ed, Boarding and Day, 13–18

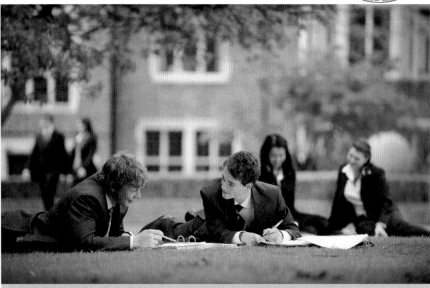

Headmaster Mr C Edwards
Worcester Road
Bromsgrove
Worcestershire
England
B61 7DU
T: 01527 579679
E: admissions@bromsgrove-school.co.uk
W: www.bromsgrove-school.co.uk

Age range 13–18
No of pupils 920; Girls 389; Boys 531
Religious denomination Christian
Founded 1553
Member of BSA, HMC, IB
Fees £14,175–£29,985

Ancient but as contemporary as tomorrow, Bromsgrove's scope is staggering: from A level to the International Baccalaureate, day to boarding, the arts to sport, pupils can soar. Utterly dedicated to the individual pupil, Bromsgrove looks to produce creative citizens with a strong moral compass and a dash of pizzazz to boot. *The Good Schools Guide* says that Bromsgrove 'inhabits the academic stratosphere' and lauds its titanic extra-curricular programme as one of the finest it has seen. Bromsgrove achieves outstanding results at both A level and IB Diploma. The extracurricular life of the School is hugely important with activities sessions every afternoon and on Saturday mornings. Pupils are encouraged to reach their highest possible level at sport, music, drama, debating, CCF and in numerous other areas. The School recently staged the schools version of Andrew Lloyd Webber's CATS to great acclaim and both boys and girls teams played hockey at national finals in 2012.

Bruton School for Girls,
Somerset, England

Girls, Day and Boarding, 11–18

BRUTON SCHOOL

FOR GIRLS

Head Mrs N Botterill
Sunny Hill
Bruton
Somerset
England
BA10 0NT
T: 01749 814400
E: admissions@brutonschool.co.uk
W: www.brutonschool.co.uk

Age range 11–18
No of pupils 262; Girls 262
Religious denomination
 Non-Denominational
Founded 1900
Member of BSA, GSA, ISA
Fees £14,031–£25,554

Set in beautiful Somerset countryside overlooking Glastonbury Tor, Bruton School for Girls aims to create a structured but challenging environment and to encourage a lively intellect, initiative, independence and respect for others. In a forward-looking and caring community with traditional values, a wide range of opportunities – academic, creative, sporting and social – is provided by a dedicated staff, allowing confident, adaptable and sensible young women to leave the school well prepared to succeed in life. Bruton School for Girls' exam results are excellent. Sport, art, drama and music thrive. Mutual respect is a corner-stone of the school and visits from prospective pupils and their parents are always welcome. Visit the website at brutonschool.co.uk or contact admissions on 01749 814400

Bryanston School, Dorset, England

Co-ed, Boarding and Day, 13–18

Head Ms S J Thomas
Bryanston
Blandford Forum
Dorset
England
DT11 0PX
T: 01258 452411
E: admissions@bryanston.co.uk
W: www.bryanston.co.uk

Age range 13–18; Boards from 13
No of pupils 678; Girls 286; Boys 392
Religious denomination Church of
England
Founded 1928
Member of HMC, IB
Fees £10,375

Occupying a magnificent mansion house amid the beautiful Dorset countryside, Bryanston aims above all to develop the all-round talents of individual pupils. A broad, flexible academic and extra-curricular programme together with an unparalleled network of adult support encourages pupils to maximise their particular abilities. Almost all pupils go on to their first choice of university, whether in the UK or abroad. Creativity, individuality and opportunity are the school's key notes, but a loving community is Bryanston's most important quality. Our aim is that Bryanstonians will leave us as well-balanced 18-year-olds, ready to go out into the wider world, to lead happy and fulfilling lives and to contribute, positively and generously. We believe a school can have no more joyful, dynamic ambition.

Canford School, Dorset, England

Co-ed, Boarding and Day, 13–18

Head Mr B Vessey
Canford Magna
Wimborne
Dorset
England
BH21 3AD
T: 01202 847207
E: admissions@canford.com
W: www.canford.com

Age range 13–18
No of pupils 635; Girls 254; Boys 381
Religious denomination Church of
England
Founded 1923
Member of HMC, ISBA
Fees £23,166–£29,640

Canford is among the top co-educational boarding schools in the country. Within its 250 acres of glorious grounds, excellent modern facilities include a Theatre, Sports Centre, Music School, 9 hole golf course, Real Tennis Court and rowing from the Boathouse on the River Stour. Academically Canford leads the way in the region at A level, and in Oxbridge entrance – 31 places in the past 2 years. Games and sports flourish, with success including an historic clean sweep of county hockey titles in 2012/2013, county rugby champions and Henley finals. The variety of extra-curricular activities include lively Arts departments and local and international community services. Ultimately, Canford seeks to educate pupils in the broadest sense of the word so that they leave as well-motivated and interesting people.

Charterhouse, Surrey, England

Boys, Boarding and Day, 13–18

Headmaster Mr R Pleming
Brook Hall, Charterhouse
Godalming
Surrey
England
GU7 2DX
T: 01483 291501
E: admissions@charterhouse.org.uk
W: www.charterhouse.org.uk

Age range 13–18; Co-ed Sixth Form
No of pupils 804; Girls 137; Boys 667
Religious denomination Christian
Founded 1611
Member of HMC, IB, ISA
Fees £27,210–£32,925

Charterhouse, with 400 years of history, is one of the leading independent schools in the world. Charterhouse remains predominantly a boarding school with around 800 pupils, taking boys from 13 and girls in the Sixth Form. The highly qualified teaching staff combines academic excellence with sympathetic and imaginative teaching to foster a love of knowledge and study. Our academic priority is not the blinkered pursuit of examination grades but the stimulation of independent enquiry and intellectual curiosity. This enables boys and girls to enter the best universities, in Britain and overseas. The School is a positive, stimulating and demanding environment, as is appropriate for the place where pupils spend some of the most important years of their lives. Our ambition is to ensure that, by providing support, encouragement and inspiration, each pupil fulfils his or her potential. We try to balance academic work with a wide range of extra-curricular opportunities, and we value sporting and cultural achievement equally.

Christ's Hospital, West Sussex, England

Co-ed, Boarding and Day, 11–18

Head Master Mr J R Franklin
Christ's Hospital
Horsham
West Sussex
England
RH13 0LJ
T: 01403 211293
E: fjd@christs-hospital.org.uk
W: www.christs-hospital.org.uk

Age range 11–18; Entry points:
Year 7, Year 9 and Sixth Form
No of pupils 860; Girls 430; Boys 430
Religious denomination Church of
England
Founded 1552
Member of HMC
Fees £28,200

Christ's Hospital is in many ways unique, offering an independent education of the highest calibre to children with academic potential, from all walks of life in a caring, boarding and day environment. Pupils' fees are assessed according to family income, so that it is a child's ability and potential to benefit from a Christ's Hospital education that determines their selection. This results in a social and cultural diversity that enriches our school community and offers our pupils unique opportunities. We believe in the benefits of a rounded and balanced education for our pupils. In practice, this means that as well as a challenging academic programme, pupils are also involved in music, art, drama, public speaking, community action and sport. The School has an impressive history of high academic achievement with an average of 10 pupils each year taking up places at Oxford or Cambridge, and 98% of leavers going on to top Universities in the UK and abroad.

City of London School, London, England

Boys, Day only, 10–18

CITY OF LONDON
SCHOOL

Headmaster Mr David Levin	**Age range** 10–18
Queen Victoria Street	**No of pupils** 920; Boys 920
London	**Religious denomination** Non-
England	Denominational
EC4V 3AL	**Founded** 1442
T: 020 7489 0291	**Member of** HMC
E: headmaster@clsb.org.uk	**Fees** £13,803
W: www.clsb.org.uk	

The ethos of the school fosters good relationships between members of the staff and the pupils. Bullying, harassment, victimisation and discrimination will not be tolerated. The school and its staff will act fairly in relation to the pupils and parents and we expect the same of pupils and parents in relation to the school. The City of London School aims to welcome talented boys from a diversity of backgrounds into a tolerant, harmonious community in which they achieve the highest academic standards, make full use of their potential and develop towards responsible adulthood. Academic achievement is very high. In 2012, 85% of GCSE entries were passed at A* or A grade. At A level, 95% of entries were passed at A* to B, with 28.9% at A*. For a central London school, this is a sporty place and the school plays 12 sports competitively. There is an on-site swimming pool, sports hall and fitness suite, and a beautiful 20-acre sports ground 30 minutes' coach drive away.

Clayesmore, Dorset, England

Co-ed, Boarding and Day, 13–18

The Headmaster Mr M G Cooke
Iwerne Minster
Blandford Forum
Dorset
England
DT11 8LL
T: 01747 812122
E: mmccafferty@clayesmore.com
W: www.clayesmore.com

Age range 13–18; Entry in Year 10
No of pupils 437; Girls 167; Boys 270
Religious denomination Church of
 England
Founded 1896
Member of BSA, CReSTeD, HMC
Fees £22,560–£30,837

Providing 'all-through' education in rural Dorset, Clayesmore was deemed 'excellent' following a recent ISI inspection that covered pupil achievement, teaching and boarding. It yields impressive A level and GCSE results from an all-ability intake and sixth formers have the pick of leading universities. Abundant extra-curricular activities and superb facilities include a sports centre, pool and astro hockey pitches. Clayesmore has its own art and music departments offering quality tuition and chances to perform. There is a wide range of scholarships available for entry in Year 9 and a number of HM Forces bursaries. With excellent teaching and Learning Support provision, the school was described as 'caring, happy and successful across all ability levels' by *The Good Schools Guide*.

Clifton College, Bristol, England
Co-ed, Boarding and Day, 13–18

Head Master Mr Mark Moore
32 College Road, Clifton
Bristol
England
BS8 3JH
T: 0117 315 7000
E: admissions@clifton-college.avon.sch.
uk
W: www.cliftoncollegeuk.com

Age range 13–18
No of pupils 710; Girls 355; Boys 355
Religious denomination Church of
England
Founded 1862
Member of BSA, HMC, ISA
Fees £21,525–£32,985

Clifton College is one of England's most famous public schools. Founded in 1862 it has always enjoyed being at the forefront of education in the UK and is superbly located in what has been described as 'the handsomest suburb in Europe', offering continuity of boarding and day education for girls and boys aged 3–18. Academic excellence (16 to Oxbridge in 2012 and 12 places offered in 2013), superb sporting and cultural facilities, magnificent buildings, a pioneering spirit and a high level of pastoral care in a friendly community characterise Clifton in the 21st Century. Ofsted and ISI award their highest accolade of 'Outstanding' for all three Schools. The city centre is within 15 minutes' walk with its universities, cinemas, museums and art galleries and such incomparable cultural benefits give Cliftonians a sense of being part of the real world.

Cobham Hall, Kent, England

Girls, Boarding and Day, 11–18

English Tradition
Global Education

Cobham Hall

Headmaster Mr Paul A Mitchell
Cobham
Gravesend
Kent
England
DA12 3BL
T: 01474 823371
E: enquiries@cobhamhall.com
W: www.cobhamhall.com

Age range 11–18
No of pupils 200; Girls 200
Religious denomination
Non-Denominational
Founded 1962
Member of AGBIS, BSA, CReSTeD, GSA,
IB, ISBA, Round
Fees £15,090–£28,734

We believe every child has the extraordinary in them, whether they know it or not. We help them find it, develop it and use it. We don't think that wanting to change the world is an unrealistic goal. Situated in 150 acres of parkland, Cobham is a magnificent mansion, once home to British nobility, now a Round Square, IB school and home to a different kind of family – 200 enthusiastic young minds, who laugh a lot and talk even more… Learning goes beyond the classroom and we encourage our girls to try new things, discover the impossible is not always so, explore the unknown and be themselves. We don't use a standard measure for extraordinariness. There is no single definition – all girls can become extraordinary. By offering diverse opportunities and experiences, we help them discover their own path.

Culford School, Suffolk, England
Co-ed, Boarding and Day, 13–18

Culford

Headmaster Mr J F Johnson-Munday	**Age range** 13–18
Culford	**No of pupils** 385; Girls 170; Boys 215
Bury St Edmunds	**Religious denomination** Methodist
Suffolk	**Founded** 1881
England	**Member of** AGBIS, BSA, HMC
IP28 6TX	**Fees** £16,500–£26,460
T: 01284 728615	
E: culfordschool@culford.co.uk	
W: www.culford.co.uk	

Culford is set in 480 acres of beautiful Suffolk parkland, located 40 minutes from Cambridge and 90 minutes from London. A friendly caring school with superb academic and sporting facilities, Culford aims to educate the whole person to deliver a well-rounded, fulfilled individual. The school's rich after-school and weekend activities programme ranges from art, music and drama through to the Combined Cadet Force and the Duke of Edinburgh's Award Scheme. Facilities include a dedicated centre for art and design technology; a superb science centre, modern studio theatre and redeveloped music school. Plans are in place for a new library providing exceptional study facilities. The sports centre boasts impressive facilities including a 25-metre indoor pool and a championship standard indoor tennis centre.

Dauntsey's School, Wiltshire, England

Co-ed, Boarding and Day, 11–18

Head Master Mr M J Lascelles
West Lavington
Devizes
Wiltshire
England
SN10 4HE
T: 01380 814500
E: info@dauntseys.org
W: www.dauntseys.org

Age range 11–18
No of pupils 775; Girls 343; Boys 432
Religious denomination Non-
Denominational
Founded 1542
Member of AGBIS, BSA, HMC, ISA, ISBA
Fees £16,050–£27,060

The Dauntsey's community is lively, creative and caring; it is a happy place with a strong family atmosphere, where friendship matters and where the courteous informality between staff and pupils is highly valued. Our pastoral framework is simple – it is one of warmth, care and discipline, where individual needs are addressed. Academic endeavour is at the heart of the School and it is expected that pupils will leave with strong examination results and a love of learning. Curiosity and a spirit of adventure are encouraged to ensure that all pupils make the most of the many opportunities on offer outside the classroom including music, drama, sport and art. We believe that if we get the environment of the School right, where courtesy, consideration for others and kindness are valued above all else, then every single one of our pupils will grow up to be confident without being arrogant, in a tolerant and harmonious atmosphere where they are happy, stimulated and inspired to succeed.

Downside School, Somerset, England

Co-ed, Boarding and Day, 13–18

Head Master Dom L Maidlow Davis
Stratton-on-the-Fosse
Bath
Somerset
England
BA3 4RJ
T: 01761 235103
E: registrar@downside.co.uk
W: www.downside.co.uk

Age range 13–18
No of pupils 360; Girls 144; Boys 216
Religious denomination Roman Catholic
Founded 1606
Member of HMC
Fees £14,154–£28,374

Downside is an independent co-educational full-boarding school and is one of England's oldest and most distinguished Catholic schools. Housed in magnificent buildings at the foot of the Mendip Hills, south of Bath in Somerset there are some 100 acres of playing fields. Academically ambitious and selective, outstanding examination results are the priority. Almost all pupils go on to the top universities in the UK, USA and Europe. Downside is proud of the outstanding level of pastoral care it provides and is well-known for its notably small tight-knit community and for the supportive relationships between the age groups. There is a wide choice of co-curricular activities and service to others is a fundamental part of life at Downside with all pupils expected to be involved in charitable and voluntary work.

Eastbourne College, East Sussex, England

Co-ed, Boarding and Day, 13–18

Eastbourne College

Headmaster Mr S P Davies
Marlborough House, Old Wish Road
Eastbourne
East Sussex
England
BN21 4JY
T: 01323 452323
E: admissions@eastbourne-college.co.uk
W: www.eastbourne-college.co.uk

Age range 13–18
No of pupils 621; Girls 266; Boys 355
Religious denomination Church of
England
Founded 1867
Member of BSA, ISA, ISBA
Fees £18,750–£28,875

Eastbourne College offers a full education that is so much more than the excellent academic results its boys and girls achieve year after year. All pupils are given every opportunity to achieve across the board: academically, in the creative arts, on the sports field, as individuals and in teams. They thrive in a welcoming and purposeful full boarding environment and develop into confident, able and responsible individuals who make life-long friends while at the College. The College is mildly selective and yet girls and boys perform in line with those from much more selective schools: in 2012 a record 87% of all A level grades were at A*–B and, for the third year in succession, the A*–B rate exceeded 80%. Scholarships are offered at Year 9 and Year 12, welcoming new scholars at a formal ceremony before they join the school and providing them with tailored development programmes throughout their school career.

EDGBASTON
HIGH SCHOOL *for* GIRLS

Edgbaston High School for Girls, West Midlands, England

Girls, Day only, 11–18

Headmistress Dr R A Weeks
Westbourne Road, Edgbaston
Birmingham
West Midlands
England
B15 3TS
T: 0121 454 5831
E: admissions@edgbastonhigh.co.uk
W: www.edgbastonhigh.co.uk

Age range 11–18
No of pupils 950; Girls 950
Religious denomination
   Non-Denominational
Founded 1876
Member of AGBIS, GSA, ISBA
Fees £4,398–£10,704

We are a lively, happy, caring community in which every girl is valued as an individual: every facet of her abilities and talents is carefully considered and developed. Our aim is to provide the highest quality of education for girls at every stage of their development. We want girls to be so stimulated and challenged during their time here that they not only meet but exceed expectations. Those expectations combine the many successes of academic and extra-curricular life with high personal standards of integrity, care and commitment. In a purposeful atmosphere for learning, personal and academic growth are enhanced by the richness of opportunity offered through a broad and progressive curriculum and stimulating extra-curricular programme.

Epsom College, Surrey, England

Co-ed, Boarding and Day, 13–18

Head Mr J Piggot
College Road
Epsom
Surrey
England
KT17 4JQ
T: 01372 821234
E: admissions@epsomcollege.org.uk
W: www.epsomcollege.org.uk

Age range 13–18; Entry at 13+ and
16+ (14+ in exceptional cases)
No of pupils 714; Girls 262; Boys 452
Religious denomination
Church of England
Founded 1855
Member of BSA, HMC
Fees £20,665–£30,222

Epsom College is one of the UK's leading independent, co-educational, boarding and day schools for pupils aged between 13 and 18. Founded as the Royal Medical Benevolent College in 1855, the College has Her Majesty Queen Elizabeth II as its patron. The magnificent original College buildings are set in an 80-acre estate on Epsom Downs. The College benefits from its close location to London, being inside the M25 yet only 30 minutes by train to central London. Both Gatwick and Heathrow airports are within easy reach and the M25 and M23 motorways are close by. Epsom College prides itself on delivering an all-round education and learning experience, where students thrive in an environment of intellectual energy, balanced by an unrivalled range of co-curricular activities. The school has a history of high academic achievement and an impressive track record of educating overseas pupils, who continue their education in the UK at top Russell Group universities. Traditional, yet forward thinking, this year will see the opening of a sister school in Malaysia.

Forest School, London, England

Co-ed, Day only, 11–18

Head Ms S J Kerr-Dineen	**Age range** 11–18
College Place	**No of pupils** 1294; Girls 641; Boys 653
London	**Religious denomination** Church of
England	England
E17 3PY	**Founded** 1834
T: 020 8520 1744	**Member of** HMC, IAPS
E: info@forest.org.uk	**Fees** £10,200–£15,081
W: www.forest.org.uk	

Surrounded by ancient forest, yet only 35 minutes from the centre of London, Forest School is an independent day school located on the edge of Epping Forest in north east London. Established in 1834, Forest boasts a beautiful campus built around the School's original Georgian and Victorian buildings.

The School comprises a Boys', Girls', and Preparatory School on a single site – and a co-educational Sixth Form. Forest's unique diamond structure allows our pupils to experience the best of all worlds. Our boys and girls (more than 1,290 in equal proportion) are taught in single-sex classes from the ages of 7–16 but come together on the co-curriculum. We believe this helps them to develop at this key stage of their development into mature, confident individuals with high expectations of what they can achieve.

Most of our pupils can expect to go on to study at some of the world's best universities. Recently described as 'outstanding' by the Independent Schools' Inspectorate, the School's academic record speaks for itself.

Framlingham College, Suffolk, England

Co-ed, Boarding and Day, 13–18

Headmaster Mr P B Taylor
College Road, Framlingham
Woodbridge
Suffolk
England
IP13 9EY
T: 01728 723789
E: admissions@framcollege.co.uk
W: www.framcollege.co.uk

Age range 13–18
No of pupils 415; Girls 175; Boys 240
Religious denomination Church of
England
Founded 1864
Member of BSA, HMC
Fees £17,372–£27,029

Framlingham College was founded in 1864 in memory of Prince Albert, the husband of Queen Victoria. Prince Albert was a stalwart supporter of education and science, as his patronage of the Great Exhibition so clearly reveals. It is fitting that his statue stands in front of the College which today is a dynamic centre of academic, cultural and sporting excellence providing fully co-educational boarding and day schooling.

The College enjoys a magnificent situation, looking out across the Mere to the twelfth-century castle. The College grounds are extensive and the original mock-Gothic buildings have been developed over the years, as a result of significant building initiatives. Its facilities now are quite exceptional.

Francis Holland School, Regent's Park NW1, London, England

Girls, Day only, 11–18

FRANCIS HOLLAND SCHOOL
REGENT'S PARK

Headmistress Mrs V M Durham
39 Ivor Place
London
England
NW1 6XR
T: 020 7723 0176
E: registrar@fhs-nw1.org.uk
W: www.francisholland.org.uk

Age range 11–18
No of pupils 460; Girls 460
Religious denomination
    Church of England
Founded 1878
Member of AGBIS, AHIS, GSA, ISA, ISBA
Fees £15,810

FHS, Regent's Park, is a happy, academic day school for girls aged 11 to 18. Within a friendly and supportive atmosphere, pupils achieve excellent examination results. All pupils transfer to universities, including Oxford and Cambridge, as well as top US institutions. Sixth formers attend weekly lectures and many complete the Extended Project. Sport, art, drama and music contribute strongly to the school's lively extra-curricular schedule. FHS has its own swimming pool and uses Regent's Park for tennis, hockey, rounders and netball. The Gloucester Wing provides additional classrooms, a fourth art studio and a performance area. There are two school orchestras, several choirs and a jazz band. The school runs more than 70 clubs and societies, such as History and Politics, fencing, water polo, Mandarin Chinese and gymnastics. Charitable initiatives include funding of a Summer Camp for local children.

Frensham Heights | Think, Create, Explore

Frensham Heights School, Surrey, England

Co-ed, Day and Boarding, 11–18

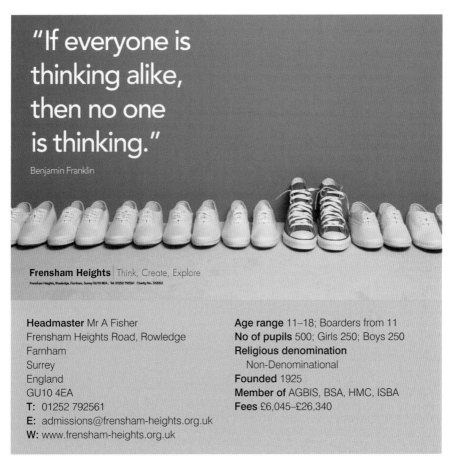

"If everyone is thinking alike, then no one is thinking."

Benjamin Franklin

Frensham Heights | Think, Create, Explore

Frensham Heights, Rowledge, Farnham, Surrey GU10 4EA . Tel. 01252 792561 Charity No. 312052

Headmaster Mr A Fisher
Frensham Heights Road, Rowledge
Farnham
Surrey
England
GU10 4EA
T: 01252 792561
E: admissions@frensham-heights.org.uk
W: www.frensham-heights.org.uk

Age range 11–18; Boarders from 11
No of pupils 500; Girls 250; Boys 250
Religious denomination
  Non-Denominational
Founded 1925
Member of AGBIS, BSA, HMC, ISBA
Fees £6,045–£26,340

Frensham Heights is a highly distinctive school in a world of education conformity. Founded in 1925, we are today acknowledged as one of the most successful liberal day and boarding schools in the country. Based in a magnificent Edwardian mansion in a hundred-plus acres of grounds, Frensham is just four miles from the pretty market town of Farnham and an hour from London. At the heart of a Frensham education is personal development and responsibility, alongside excellent academic achievement. We are awarded one of the first Arts council Gold Artmark awards, confirming our pre-eminence as a school where creative thought permeates the whole curriculum. We offer a wide range of GCSE, AS and A level subjects as well as extensive extra-curricular activities and a challenging outdoor education programme.

Glenalmond College,

Perth and Kinross, Scotland

Co-ed, Boarding and Day, 12–18

Glenalmond College
inspiring learning

The Warden Mr G Woods
Glenalmond
Perth
Perth and Kinross
Scotland
PH1 3RY
T: 01738 842000
E: registrar@glenalmondcollege.co.uk
W: www.glenalmondcollege.co.uk

Age range 12–18
No of pupils 381; Girls 151; Boys 230
Religious denomination Episcopalian
Founded 1847
Member of AGBIS, BSA, HMC, ISBA, SCIS
Fees £14,970–£29,295

Glenalmond College has a well-justified reputation as one of the UK's top boarding schools, with a tradition of excellence and achievement.

The academic focus of the school is clear, with over half of Glenalmond's leavers getting places at Russell Group universities, the top 24 universities in the UK. 5–10% of pupils each year achieve places at Oxford and Cambridge, and every pupil is helped throughout their school career to recognise and develop their academic strengths. All pupils study for GCSEs and A levels, with a curriculum spanning 24 subjects in the Sixth Form offering an excellent basis for entry to university and higher education.

As well as developing academic potential, Glenalmond encourages its pupils in other areas too. Over 145 sports, activities, clubs and societies are on offer. On the sporting front, the school's Athlete Development Programme ensures that the school's young sportsmen and women benefit from the best coaching available.

Gordonstoun School, Morayshire, Scotland

Co-ed, Boarding and Day, 8–18

Principal Mr Simon Reid
Elgin
Moray
Morayshire
Scotland
IV30 5RF
T: 01343 837837
E: admissions@gordonstoun.org.uk
W: www.gordonstoun.org.uk

Age range 8–18
No of pupils 589; Girls 244;
Boys 345
Religious denomination
Non-Denominational
Founded 1934
Member of BSA, Round, SCIS
Fees £11,970–£28,944

Gordonstoun is one of the few remaining full boarding schools in the UK. Situated on the Moray Coast, yet close to two international airports, students can take full advantage of its spectacular location. The educational programme is fully inclusive with all students being offered a programme of study based on four distinct educational principles: Challenge, Service, Internationalism and Responsibility. Students are challenged academically, physically and emotionally and the opportunities available to them – some of which are genuinely unique – provide them with significant life-shaping experiences. The school motto, Plus Est en Vous (There's more in you) is central to our ethos and underpins every aspect of the curriculum and its delivery.

Haileybury, Hertfordshire, England

Co-ed, Boarding and Day, 11–18

The Master Mr J S Davies
Haileybury
Hertford
Hertfordshire
England
SG13 7PU
T: 01992 706353
E: registrar@haileybury.com
W: www.haileybury.com

Age range 11–18; Entry at 11+, 13+ and
16+. Occasionally places are available
at 14+. Flexi-boarding available at 11+
only; choice of full boarding or day once
pupils reach 13+.
No of pupils 757; Girls 317; Boys 440
Religious denomination Church of
England
Founded 1862
Member of BSA, HMC, IB
Fees £14,145–£28,341

Haileybury is a leading independent school located 20 miles north of central London in 500 acres of beautiful rural Hertfordshire. The spectacular grounds are home to outstanding facilities, excellent teaching and superb pastoral care for our community of pupils. Haileybury is proud of its history, tradition, community and values, taking the best from the past while looking to the future. Academic rigour and outstanding co-curricular provision provide exceptional opportunities and a truly all-round education, allowing our pupils to discover enduring passions and talents. The school offers a dedicated Lower School (Years 7 and 8), a unique Year 9 curriculum, a wide range of I/GCSEs and the choice of IB Diploma or A levels in the Sixth Form. We warmly invite you to visit to discover what life at Haileybury has to offer and why your child will flourish here.

Hampton School, Middlesex, England

Boys, Day only, 11–18

Head Master Mr K Knibbs
Hanworth Road
Hampton
Middlesex
England
TW12 3HD
T: 020 8979 5526
E: admissions@hamptonschool.org.uk
W: www.hamptonschool.org.uk

Age range 11–18; Entry at 11+, 13+ and
16+
No of pupils 1200; Boys 1200
Religious denomination
Non-Denominational
Founded 1556
Member of HMC
Fees £15,990

One of the UK's top-performing schools, Hampton provides an outstanding boys-only education combining academic excellence with exceptional pastoral care. Situated in spacious grounds in the suburbs of west London, the School is easily accessible from central London, Middlesex and Surrey. Teaching is challenging, innovative and tailored to suit boys' learning styles. Virtually all boys go on to elite universities (32 Oxbridge places in 2013).The School has a much-envied reputation for sport and offers first-class coaching, superb on-site playing fields and state-of-the art 3G area. Strengths are cricket, football, rowing, rugby, tennis and chess. One of only a few Steinway Schools in the UK; creative life is exceptional and a new Performing Arts centre supports an impressive programme of music and drama.

Harrogate Ladies' College,

North Yorkshire, England

Girls, Boarding and Day, 11–18

Headmistress Mrs R J Wilkinson
Clarence Drive
Harrogate
North Yorkshire
England
HG1 2QG
T: 01423 504543
E: enquire@hlc.org.uk
W: www.hlc.org.uk

Age range 11–18
No of pupils 350; Girls 350
Religious denomination
   Church of England
Founded 1893
Member of AGBIS, GSA
Fees £13,950–£29,670

Harrogate Ladies' College combines the best aspects of a traditional British education with the skills, qualifications and modern outlook needed by today's students. We are an academically successful school with an award winning Business School and provide outstanding provision of pastoral care. The school is situated in the heart of the beautiful spa town of Harrogate in rural North Yorkshire and has good rail and road links with easy access to the local Leeds/Bradford airport. Boarding houses are arranged vertically from U3 (Year 7) to L6 (Year 12). Upper Sixth Formers enjoy a greater sense of freedom in their own accommodation called 'Tower House'. Each House has a Housemistress and an Assistant Housemistress who are responsible for the well-being of the girls. All students in the Sixth Form have private studies in school with internet access.

Heathfield School, Ascot, Berkshire, England

Girls, Boarding, 11–18

Head Mrs J Heywood
London Road
Ascot
Berkshire
England
SL5 8BQ
T: 01344 898343
E: registrar@heathfieldschool.net
W: www.heathfieldschool.net

Age range 11–18
No of pupils 200; Girls 200
Religious denomination
Church of England
Founded 1899
Member of AEGIS, AGBIS, ASCL, BSA,
GSA, NAHT
Fees £30,348–£31,041

Heathfield is a renowned girls' boarding school set in stunning grounds just 45 minutes from central London. The school's strength is in its size: as a small school, it is able to offer an unrivalled emphasis on nurturing each girl so that she can achieve the very best she can. Heathfield's aim is to help all girls get the most out of life by providing the finest intellectual stimulation, physical challenges and pastoral care. The school was recently recognised by both the ISI and the national media for its outstanding pastoral care. Each pupil is a key part of an exciting community: Heathfield believes time spent outside the classroom is just as important as the time spent in it and has a varied and exciting extra-curricular programme. Academically, girls are guided and monitored by a personal tutor.

Heathfield School for Girls, Middlesex, England

Girls, Day only, 11–18

Head Mistress Mrs A Stevens
Beaulieu Drive
Pinner
Middlesex
England
HA5 1NB
T: 020 8868 2346
E: j.moseley@hea.gdst.net
W: www.heathfield.gdst.net

Age range 11–18
No of pupils 433; Girls 433
Religious denomination
Non-Denominational
Founded 1900
Member of AGBIS, GDST, GSA, ISBA
Fees £8,628–£14,235

A unique and exceptional school where each child is valued and cherished; a home where dreams are inspired and nurtured; and a family who together build solid foundations for outstanding futures. We identify the strengths of each child and develop their raw talents by supporting, enthusing and challenging each step of the way. This personalised approach has reaped rewards with outstanding examination results year on year. Whether the end goal is to be accepted into a leading university or to enter the world of work, we equip each girl with the knowledge and confidence that they require to succeed with an education that is innovative, challenging and enriching. We benefit from being a part of the Girls' Day School Trust, a network of 25 schools and 2 academies, and a leader and pioneer in girls' education.

Hurtwood House, Surrey, England

Co-ed, Boarding and Day, 16–18

The Headmaster Mr CM Jackson	**Age range** 16–18
Holmbury St Mary	**No of pupils** 330; Girls 165; Boys 165
Dorking	**Religious denomination**
Surrey	Non-Denominational
England	**Founded** 1970
RH5 6NU	**Member of** BSA, ISA
T: 01483 279000	**Fees** £12,250–£14,087
E: info@hurtwood.net	
W: www.hurtwoodhouse.com	

Hurtwood House is a boarding school with a difference – a big difference! Although it has all the facilities of a typical public school, it specialises exclusively in the Sixth Form. Changing schools at 16 opens up a whole new world of fresh experiences and Hurtwood provides the perfect stepping-stone between school and university. Hurtwood House is young, exciting and dynamic and, it is exceptionally creative with drama, media, art, textiles, dance, music and singing to die for. It has a particularly wide range of A levels ranging from traditional academic subjects such as Maths, Sciences, Modern Languages, Economics etc, plus an outstanding selection from the creative and performing arts. Hurtwood has a fantastic academic record with 67% achieving A*/A in 2013.

Kelly College, Devon, England

Co-ed, Day and Boarding, 11–18

The Headmaster Dr GRW Hawley
Parkwood Road
Tavistock
Devon
England
PL19 0HZ
T: 01822 813100
E: admissions@kellycollege.com
W: www.kellycollege.com

Age range 11–18
No of pupils 330; Girls 146; Boys 184
Religious denomination Christian
Founded 1877
Member of BSA, HMC
Fees £5,985–£26,985

Kelly College is a friendly, co-educational boarding and day school, providing a fulfilling, all-round education, located on a stunning 65-acre site overlooking the Tavy Valley and Dartmoor National Park. We offer a seamless transition from Kelly College Preparatory School, for ages 3 to 11, to Kelly College, for ages 11 to 18. Our principal aims are to encourage the pursuit of excellence and the development of the whole person, in nurturing surroundings. Pupils achieve their true potential within a supportive environment, developing their individual talents. We balance a high standard of academic schooling with a strong commitment to co-curricular activities such as the Combined Cadet Force, Duke of Edinburgh's Award and Ten Tors Challenge. Scholarships, exhibitions and awards are available in many areas.

Kent College Canterbury, Kent, England

Co-ed, Day and Boarding, 11–18

KENT COLLEGE
——— CANTERBURY ———

Head Master Dr DJ Lamper
Whitstable Road, Blean
Canterbury
Kent
England
CT2 9DT
T: 01227 763231
E: registrar@kentcollege.co.uk
W: www.kentcollege.com

Age range 11–18
No of pupils 474; Girls 223; Boys 251
Religious denomination Methodist
Founded 1885
Member of BSA, IB, IBSCA
Fees £14,998–£29,736

Kent College is situated in an idyllic spot over looking Canterbury. Access is easy not only for the major airports but also for the high speed train link to London and Europe. It is predominantly a day school but with the benefit of boarding. 'Boarding is at the Heart of the School!' Ofsted. We offer IB alongside A levels in the Sixth Form, giving our students access to the top universities both here and abroad. Academic results are excellent and we are regularly in the top 100 for our A level results and in the top 10 nationally for IB. It is the ability to fit the timetable to the child with our bespoke timetabling, which enables pupils to realise their full potential. 64 activities, our own school farm and regular trips mean there is something for everyone!

King Edward's School, Bath,

Bath & North East Somerset, England

Co-ed, Day only, 11–18

KING
EDWARD'S
SCHOOL
BATH

Head Mr Martin Boden
North Road
Bath
Bath & North East Somerset
England
BA2 6HU
T: 01225 4643134
E: senior@kesbath.com
W: www.kesbath.com.uk

Age range 11–18
No of pupils 979; Girls 359; Boys 620
Religious denomination
    Non-Denominational
Founded 1552
Member of HMC, ISBA

King Edward's School, Bath is an independent co-educational day school for children aged from 3 to 18 years. Founded in 1552 by King Edward VI; King Edward's School is one of the country's leading independent schools. Academic performance is one of the School's many strengths; with results at A level, AS level and GCSE placing the School in the premier tier of schools in the country. Pupils go on to the top universities and successful careers. A recent ISI report judged the School's pastoral care to be 'outstanding'. King Edward's has a strong reputation for sporting excellence, as well as being strong in the creative arts; music, drama and art. The School offers an extensive extra-curricular programme. The facilities are first rate and the School continues to invest in new developments to enhance the already excellent provision.

King Henry VIII School, West Midlands, England

Co-ed, Day only, 11–18

Headmaster Mr J Slack
Warwick Road
Coventry
West Midlands
England
CV3 6AQ
T: 024 7627 1111
E: info@khviii.net
W: www.khviii.com

Age range 11–18
No of pupils 789; Girls 345; Boys 444
Religious denomination Christian
Founded 1545
Member of HMC, NAHT
Fees £9,816

Highly regarded throughout Warwickshire and the West Midlands, King Henry VIII School has been providing a first class education since its foundation in 1545. Proudly co-educational for over 40 years and boasting a bright, diverse and friendly student body, it is a school where each child is able to find their talents and to flourish. The excellent neighbouring Prep School allows a smooth educational journey from 3 to 18 years of age. Academic results are amongst the best in the region whilst fees are remarkably good value. Children flock to the school locally but the two-minute walk from Coventry train station also attracts many from further afield. With wonderful, supportive teachers, small class sizes and a spacious, leafy campus, the school is a model of the best that independent education can offer.

KING'S BRUTON
Deo Juvante

King's Bruton, Somerset, England
Co-ed, Boarding and Day, 13–18

Headmaster Mr Ian S Wilmshurst
The Plox
Bruton
Somerset
England
BA10 0ED
T: 01749 814200
E: office@kingsbruton.com
W: www.kingsbruton.com

Age range 13–18; Entry at 13 and into 6th from
No of pupils 334; Girls 122; Boys 212
Religious denomination Christian
Founded 1519
Member of BSA, CReSTeD, HMC, ISBA
Fees £19,422–£27,135

King's Bruton had its best A level results on record in 2012, while its teaching, learning and pastoral care was judged 'outstanding' in its most recent inspection by the Independent Schools Inspectorate (ISI). In the A2 exam results, the percentage of grades at A*–B was 77.2% which surpassed the previous highest percentage (74.3% in 2010). The percentage of grades A*– A was 43.5% and the pass rate was 100%. Nine pupils achieved straight A grades. As well as identifying the School's outstanding academic and pastoral strengths, noting the way pupils 'aim high and achieve well', the ISI report also singled out the pupils' excellent personal development, describing them as 'confident, relaxed and articulate.' The School offers a wide range of extra-curricular activities, priding itself on strong and competitive Sport, thriving Music and Drama departments, and a wide range of other opportunities to learn and experience new skills, pastimes and hobbies.

King's Ely, Cambridgeshire, England

Co-ed, Day and Boarding, 13–18

Head Mrs S E Freestone	**Age range** 13–18; Boarding from age 8
Ely	**No of pupils** 436; Girls 185; Boys 251
Cambridgeshire	**Religious denomination** Church of
England	England
CB7 4EW	**Founded** 970
T: 01353 660700	**Member of** HMC, SHMIS
E: admissions@kingsely.org	**Fees** £18,009–£26,070
W: www.kingsely.org	

Founded in 970 and re-founded in 1541 by King Henry VIII, King's Ely is situated in the heart of the cathedral city of Ely. Much of the school is housed in the buildings of the old Benedictine monastery, which include the 14th-century Monastic Barn (now the school dining hall) and the Porta (monastery gateway), now the school library. Ely Cathedral serves as the school chapel. In the last 10 years there has been extensive development including a new music school and recital hall, art complex and all-weather pitch. The renovated Old Palace became a Sixth Form Study Centre in 2012. King's Ely provides a challenging and inspiring learning environment and is a recipient of the coveted NACE award for the excellent standard of teaching and learning. Courtesy, respect and integrity are strongly encouraged.

Kingswood School,

Bath & North East Somerset, England

Co-ed, Boarding and Day, 11–18

Head Master Mr S Morris
Lansdown
Bath
Bath & North East Somerset
England
BA1 5RG
T: 01225 734200
E: enquiries@kingswood.bath.sch.uk
W: www.kingswood.bath.sch.uk

Age range 11–18
No of pupils 708; Girls 327; Boys 381
Religious denomination Methodist
Founded 1748
Member of AGBIS, BSA, HMC, ISBA
Fees £12,177–£26,241

Kingswood is a very special place; a historically significant school founded in 1748 by John Wesley, it continues to provide a happy, caring and disciplined environment based on strong Christian principles. With a commitment to make a real difference to every child who passes through we strive for all-round excellence. The Headmaster and Governors place great emphasis on the quality of relationships; individuality and innovation; these are valued and a sense of service is encouraged. An atmosphere of tolerance, understanding and inclusion permeates teaching and learning to enable every child to flourish. There are excellent facilities for boarding and day pupils within one of the most beautiful locations in the South West of England being only 10 minutes' walk from the World Heritage City of Bath and easy travel links to London.

Lancing College, West Sussex, England

Co-ed, Boarding and Day, 13–18

The Head Master Mr J W J Gillespie	**Age range** 13–18; Additional intake into
Lancing	Sixth Form (Year 12)
West Sussex	**No of pupils** 529; Girls 175; Boys 354
England	**Religious denomination** Church of
BN15 0RW	England
T: 01273 465805	**Founded** 1848
E: admissions@lancing.org.uk	**Member of** BSA, HMC
W: www.lancingcollege.co.uk	**Fees** £7,260–£31,020

This historic senior school has a broad academic intake but achieves consistently strong results and outstanding value-added at A level; the average A*–B grades for the last nine years is 83%. University destinations include Oxbridge and those within the Russell Group. Its beautiful campus is set in 550 acres of Sussex downland; facilities are excellent and pastoral care exceptional. Lancing is renowned for the quality of its music, drama and art and for its welcoming and exhilarating atmosphere. Numerous sporting and cultural activities are available for students to delve into, opening doors to new talents and life-long interests. An emphasis is placed on individuals developing at their own pace. The College Farm, CCF, Duke of Edinburgh's Award, Outreach and overseas trips further enrich pupils' lives.

Leighton Park School, Berkshire, England

Co-ed, Boarding and Day, 11–18

Leighton Park
School

Head Mr D N Williams
Shinfield Road
Reading
Berkshire
England
RG2 7ED
T: 0118 987 9600
E: info@leightonpark.com
W: www.leightonpark.com

Age range 11–18
No of pupils 480; Girls 190; Boys 290
Religious denomination Quaker
Founded 1890
Member of AGBIS, BSA, HMC, IB, IBSCA, ISA, ISBA, SHMIS
Fees £15,759–£29,730

Set in a beautiful 65-acre park on the outskirts of Reading, Leighton Park School is an independent co-educational day and boarding school where students from ages 11 to 18 can live, learn and grow. High academic standards and a richly diverse extra-curricular programme provide students with the tools they need to reach their full potential, both academically and as individuals. Students are encouraged to seek out and nurture all of their talents within a purposeful academic environment and are prepared for life beyond school by a holistic approach, inspiring teachers and renowned pastoral care. Founded on the Quaker values of equality, integrity, respect, peace, truth, simplicity and sustainability, it is the ideal environment in which to think, reflect and learn.

The Leys School, Cambridgeshire, England

Co-ed, Boarding and Day, 11–18

Headmaster Mr M Priestley	**Age range** 11–18
Fen Causeway	**No of pupils** 550; Girls 220; Boys 330
Cambridge	**Religious denomination** Methodist
Cambridgeshire	**Founded** 1875
England	**Member of** HMC, ISA
CB2 7AD	**Fees** £13,185–£27,780
T: 01223 508900	
E: office@theleys.net	
W: www.theleys.net	

The Leys is one of England's premier independent schools. Established in 1875, the school offers a blend of traditional values and a forward-looking approach to education, to prepare young people for the challenges and excitements which lie ahead at University and beyond.

Set on the edge of the beautiful and stimulating city of Cambridge, The Leys is a close-knit, friendly community in which pastoral care is seen as a top priority. The confidence which our pupils gain from this encouraging family atmosphere enables them to fulfil their potential in work and play.

Being a smaller independent school (approximately 550 pupils) The Leys is able to offer more individual attention. This makes it easier to discover what motivates each child and, in so doing, to nurture their abilities – whatever they might be.

The teaching of Science and the Performing Arts is being further enhanced at The Leys by the opening of Great Hall (September 2013). It will house 3 new science laboratories, a rooftop outdoor experiment space, drama and dance studios and a 320 seat Theatre.

Lichfield Cathedral School, Staffordshire, England

Co-ed, Day and Boarding, 11–18

Headmaster Mr D Coran
The Palace, The Close
Lichfield
Staffordshire
England
WS13 7LH
T: 01543 306170
E: thepalace@lichfieldcathedralschool.com
W: www.lichfieldcathedralschool.com

Age range 11–18; Boarding for boy
  choristers only
No of pupils 201; Girls 83; Boys 118
Religious denomination
  Church of England
Founded 1942
Member of AGBIS, BSA, ISBA, SHMIS
Fees £11,130–£17,670

Set in the historic Cathedral Close, Lichfield Cathedral School provides independent education for girls and boys aged 3 to 18, from Pre-School to Sixth Form. Class sizes are kept small and specialist teaching is provided from an early age. The school offers a broad curriculum, combined with traditional values, a Christian ethos and first-class teaching. Primarily a day school, boarding is available for 20 boy choristers. Whilst the school holds an exceptional reputation for music education, particularly for boy and girl choristers, there is no specific type of student at LCS: academics, artists, athletes and the adventurous are all welcome. Plenty of extra-curricular opportunities ensure that pupils are typically well-rounded, dynamic and ambitious.

Llandovery College, Carmarthenshire, Wales

Co-ed, Boarding and Day, 11–18

Llandovery
College

Warden & Headmaster Mr Guy Aylling	**Age range** 11–18
Queensway	**No of pupils** 277; Girls 100; Boys 177
Llandovery	**Religious denomination** Church in Wales
Carmarthenshire	**Founded** 1847
Wales	**Member of** SHMIS
SA20 0EE	
T: 01550 723000	
E: admissions@llandoverycollege.com	
W: www.llandoverycollege.com	

Llandovery College is one of Wales's most respected independent boarding schools set in 45 acres of safe green, wooded campus and surrounded by stunning countryside. The area is renowned for its friendliness, safe environment and low traffic and pollution levels. The school is a wonderful mix of traditional and modern with a truly global approach to education and an international reputation for sport. Mellow old buildings blend with modern teaching faculties and pupils have access to the very latest technology and superb facilities. Academic excellence is our primary aim and at the heart of Llandovery College's ethos is the emphasis on the importance of individual effort, talent and attainment.

Lord Wandsworth College, Hampshire, England

Co-ed, Boarding and Day, 11–18

Headmaster Mr F Q Livingstone
Long Sutton
Hook
Hampshire
England
RG29 1TB
T: 01256 862201
E: admissions@lordwandsworth.org
W: www.lordwandsworth.org

Age range 11–18
No of pupils 530; Girls 174; Boys 356
Religious denomination Non-
 Denominational
Founded 1922
Member of BSA, HMC
Fees £18,240–£27,090

The safe, rural campus community and the College's Foundation of supporting children who have lost one or both parents, as well as a long tradition of pupils achieving academic results beyond expectations, is what sets it apart from other schools in the area.

The school has a family friendly focus and it provides a truly 'all round' education for children of varying academic backgrounds – from the very brightest to those who need a little more support. Sport, music, drama, cultural and outdoor pursuits all play a vital part in the educational mix. Developing each student's character strengths is central to our ethos.

We are ideal for busy, working families as weekly, full and flexi boarding options are all on offer but day pupils are equally welcome.

Do come and visit us to find out more – you will be assured a warm welcome.

MALVERN ST JAMES
GIRLS' SCHOOL

Malvern St James Girls' School,
Worcestershire, England

Girls, Boarding and Day, 11–18

Headmistress Mrs P Woodhouse
15 Avenue Road
Great Malvern
Worcestershire
England
WR14 3BA
T: 01684 584624
E: registrar@malvernstjames.co.uk
W: www.malvernstjames.co.uk

Age range 11–18
No of pupils 400; Girls 400
Religious denomination Church of
England
Founded 1852
Member of BSA, GSA, NAHT

Malvern St James Girls' School offers first class education, especially for girls. As one of the UK's finest independent girls' boarding schools, we are proud of our history, heritage, cutting-edge facilities and resources which ensure a highly distinctive, innovative education is offered from Reception through to Sixth Form, all within our stunning integrated campus. Many girls enjoy full, weekly or flexi boarding, as suits the lifestyle of each pupil and her family. The Malvern St James community of 400 girls thrive within our positive, purposeful environment, which cultivates creativity and bold-thinking. Inspiring and equipping girls for the modern world, MSJ's opportunities identify and maximise all talents. Exploration and extra-curricular enrichment is key to the MSJ Education, and in our School everything is possible! Scholarships are offered for 11+, 13+ and Sixth Form entry for excellence in Art, Academia, Drama, Music, Riding and Sports.

mgs Founded 1515 | The Manchester Grammar School

The Manchester Grammar School,

Greater Manchester, England

Boys, Day only, 11–18

Head Dr Martin Boulton
Old Hall Lane
Manchester
Greater Manchester
England
M13 0XT
T: 0161 224 7201
E: admissions@mgs.org
W: www.mgs.org

Age range 11–18
No of pupils 1500; Boys 1500
Religious denomination
    Non-Denominational
Founded 1515
Member of AGBIS, HMC, ISA
Fees £10,545

MGS is one of the very best academic schools for boys in the UK, unashamedly a meritocracy, with a record of examination success unequalled north of London and Oxford. Our students study at the most prestigious universities in the World, including this year 28 to Oxford and Cambridge, and nine to the American Ivy Leagues. All MGS boys are very clever, but beyond that, they are a delightfully eclectic mixture representing every creed, ethnicity, religious and socio-economic background. They have excellent opportunities to enjoy sport, drama, art, music and any one of our 192 clubs and societies, with many going on to compete at local, national and international level in their chosen passion. To discover more about MGS do visit our website at mgs.org or contact Kath Heathcote k.t.heathcote@mgs.org, or 0161 224 7201 Ext 234.

Merchiston Castle School,

Lothian, Scotland

Boys, Boarding and Day, 13–18

Head Mr A R Hunter

294 Colinton Road

Edinburgh

Lothian

Scotland

EH13 0PU

T: +44 00 131 312 2204

E: externalrelations@merchiston.co.uk

W: www.merchiston.co.uk

Age range 13–18

No of pupils 470; Boys 470

Religious denomination
Inter-Denominational

Founded 1833

Member of BSA, CReSTeD, ISBA, SCIS, SHMIS

Fees £17,070–£26,655

Merchiston Castle School is the only boys' independent boarding school in Scotland and is renowned for providing a superb all-round education.

Set in 100 acres of beautiful parkland, Merchiston's goal is to help every boy reach his full potential and leave the School ready for the world. Merchiston is consistently in the top flight of UK independent schools and was named the Top Scottish School for A levels in 2011 and 2012. Pupils' applications to the most prestigious colleges continue to meet with success including those to the Russell Group Universities and Oxbridge.

Within fantastic facilities, there are over 20 sports on offer which cater for all interests and abilities. The School established Scotland's first tennis academy in 2007 and more recently its own golf academy. Merchiston is currently represented at national and international level in many sports including athletics, cricket and rugby.

Merchiston was rated 'Excellent' in all areas by the Care Inspectorate in 2012.

Oakham School, Rutland, England

Co-ed, Boarding and Day, 13–18

Headmaster Mr Nigel M Lashbrook
Chapel Close, Market Place
Oakham
Rutland
England
LE15 6DT
T: 01572 758758
E: admissions@oakham.rutland.sch.uk
W: www.oakham.rutland.sch.uk

Age range 13–18
No of pupils 1050; Girls 505; Boys 545
Religious denomination
　Church of England
Founded 1584
Member of BSA, HMC, IB, IBSCA, ISBA
Fees £15,615–£29,355

Oakham is a boarding and day school for boys and girls aged 10 to 18, offering a choice of IB or A levels in the sixth form. Friendly and unpretentious, Oakham achieves impressive academic results at A level and GCSE; we are one of the UK's Top Ten IB schools. Our strength lies in challenging every individual to exceed his or her expectations through encouragement, pastoral support and a diversity of opportunity. Our Learning Habits at Oakham initiative develops lifelong learning skills and underpins all our teaching. Every pupil is valued and motivated to work hard. Sport, music, drama and the arts flourish. Our extensive activities programme includes voluntary action both locally and overseas. Oakhamians are warm, approachable but confident and determined young people. It is a very exciting place to be.

Old Palace of John Whitgift School,
Surrey, England

Girls, Day only, 10–18

Head Mrs C Jewel
Old Palace Road
Croydon
Surrey
England
CR0 1AX
T: 020 8688 2027
E: schooloffice@oldpalace.croydon.sch.uk
W: www.oldpalace.croydon.sch.uk

Age range 10–18
No of pupils 1211; Girls 800; Boys 411
Religious denomination Church of
England
Founded 1889
Member of AGBIS, GSA
Fees £9,228–£12,480

Founded in 1889, Old Palace a unique school in an exceptional and inspiring setting steeped in history dating back to 896AD. It is this setting that enables us to identify, encourage and nurture the special qualities of each and every individual entrusted to us. Our surroundings also stimulate girls to develop and flourish in ways beyond the reach of a conventional education. For example, not every girls' school in the country can boast the opportunity to sing cathedral repertoire every week at Croydon Minster, our next door neighbour at Old Palace. Old Palace is blessed with magnificent buildings, enthusiastic, highly motivated staff and a sound ethos of social awareness. A member of the Whitgift Foundation since 1992, the school offers a generous bursary and scholarship scheme for successful applicants.

Our Lady's Abingdon School,
Oxfordshire, England

Co-ed, Day only, 11–18

Head Mr S Oliver
Radley Road
Abingdon
Oxfordshire
England
OX14 3PS
T: 01235 524658
E: office@olab.org.uk
W: www.olab.org.uk

Age range 11–18
No of pupils 383; Girls 288; Boys 95
Religious denomination Roman Catholic
Founded 1860
Member of AGBIS, IAPS, ISA, ISBA,
SHMIS
Fees £6,981–£11,832

OLA is a Catholic school that also welcomes pupils from other Christian denominations and faiths. Praised in 2010 by the Independent Schools Inspectorate for outstanding pastoral care & excellent extra-curricular activities, OLA also achieves impressive academic results. Please see website for details. Small classes make for an excellent pupil/teacher ratio, encouraging pupils to feel inspired and valued. Most Sixth Formers obtain a place at their first choice university, including Oxford, Cambridge & Russell Group universities. Pupils broaden their horizons & develop self-confidence through an extensive enrichment programme. Facilities include a 25m indoor swimming pool, multi-purpose auditorium, Library, seven Science laboratories, Music Centre, two ICT suites, Art and Drama studios, Sports Hall, courts and playing field. Among sports played are netball, rugby, hockey, football, swimming, cricket, athletics, tennis and sailing.

PRIOR PARK
COLLEGE
BATH

Prior Park College, Bath & North East Somerset, England

Co-ed, Boarding and Day, 13–18

Headmaster Mr J Murphy-O'Connor

Ralph Allen Drive

Bath

Bath & North East Somerset

England

BA2 5AH

T: 01225 835353

E: admissions@priorpark.co.uk

W: www.thepriorfoundation.com

Age range 13–18

No of pupils 570; Girls 255; Boys 315

Religious denomination Roman Catholic

Founded 1830

Member of BSA, HMC, IAPS

Fees £12,657–£25,434

Situated on a beautiful 57-acre site overlooking the World Heritage City of Bath, the College has a thriving Catholic Christian community which is ecumenical in spirit. It has outstanding facilities with over 20 music, drama and dance productions held in the magnificent Chapel, John Wood Chapel, Julian Slade Theatre and Mackintosh Studio each year. A broad and balanced sporting curriculum helps to promote sporting excellence and sporting opportunities for all. Prior Park A level students achieve outstanding results year on year with over one-fifth gaining 3 A grades or better. The College was top equal in the area for GCSE in 2012, with its 5 good GCSE percentage at 98%, placing it in the top quartile in the country. Also in 2012, for the third consecutive year, Prior students achieved truly outstanding results in the EPQ (Extended Project Qualification). Prior prides itself on the strength of its teacher/student relationships which engender the students' best efforts and earnest commitment to learning.

Prior's Field, Surrey, England

Girls, Day and Boarding, 11–18

Headmistress Mrs J Roseblade
Priorsfield Road, Hurtmore
Godalming
Surrey
England
GU7 2RH
T: 01483 810551
E: registrar@priorsfieldschool.com
W: www.priorsfieldschool.com

Age range 11–18; Main points of entry are
at 11+, followed by 13+ and 16+.
No of pupils 450; Girls 450
Religious denomination
Non-Denominational
Founded 1902
Member of BSA, GSA
Fees £15,855–£25,575

'Nothing is ever ordinary at Prior's Field' (Parent). The school pursues a broad and innovative curriculum, with over 20 subjects offered at A level. Results are excellent: in 2012, 46% of A level grades were A*–A; 73% A*–B. Pupils participate in over 50 termly clubs, including silver smithing, philosophy, riding and Greenpower engineering. An Elite Tennis Academy and all-weather sports pitch are recent additions to superb facilities. In September 2013 a new three-storey building opened, siting the Creative Arts subjects together. A boarding and day school, Prior's Field offers full, weekly and flexi boarding. A highly supportive university application process ensures that all girls move to higher education. Over 80% gained first choice places in 2012, the majority at Russell Group universities.

Reading Blue Coat School, Berkshire, England

Boys, Day only, 11–18

Headmaster Mr M J Windsor
Holme Park, Sonning Lane on-Thames
Sonning
Reading
Berkshire
England
RG4 6SU
T: 0118 944 1005
E: reception@rbcs.org.uk
W: www.rbcs.org.uk

Age range 11–18; Girls 16–18
No of pupils 718; Girls 75; Boys 643
Religious denomination Church of
England
Founded 1646
Member of AGBIS, HMC, SHMIS
Fees £13,470

Reading Blue Coat School is an independent school for boys 11–18, with a co-educational Sixth Form. The school is situated on a 46-acre site by the Thames in the village of Sonning. Facilities include a new 23-classroom teaching block and art department, an all-purpose sports centre, a dedicated Sixth Form Centre, a boathouse on the Thames, a cricket pavilion and an indoor swimming pool. While academic success is important at Blue Coat, we offer a generous co-curricular provision in both sport and the Arts, as well as a Combined Cadet Force, D of E and an extensive programme of trips and visits.

Royal Grammar School, Guildford,

Surrey, England

Boys, Day only, 11–18

Headmaster Dr J M Cox
High Street
Guildford
Surrey
England
GU1 3BB
T: 01483 880600
E: office@rgs-guildford.co.uk
W: www.rgs-guildford.co.uk

Age range 11–18
No of pupils 900; Boys 900
Religious denomination
Non-Denominational
Founded 1509
Member of HMC
Fees £14,010–£14,325

Located in the centre of the historic town of Guildford, the RGS is an independent day school. As a flagship for boys' education, the School has a national reputation for academic excellence; the RGS is consistently one of the top five boys' schools in the country at both A level and GCSE and is extremely proud of its Oxbridge record: over 200 offers have been achieved in the last six years. The School prides itself on its traditional values of decency and respect, supported by outstanding pastoral care. RGS boys have the opportunity to experience the widest range of enriching activities and extra-curricular opportunities which provides them with a broad and balanced education. The boys enjoy learning in an environment which allows them fully to realise their natural potential.

The Royal High School, Bath,

Bath & North East Somerset, England

Girls, Day and Boarding, 11–18

Headmistress Mrs Rebecca Dougall

Lansdown Road

Bath

Bath & North East Somerset

England

BA1 5SZ

T: 01225 313877

E: royalhigh@bat.gdst.net

W: www.royalhighbath.gdst.net

Age range 11–18

No of pupils 680; Girls 680

Religious denomination
Non-Denominational

Founded 1864

Member of GDST, GSA, IB

Laughter and a lifelong love of learning, collaboration and camaraderie, drive and determination, inspiration and involvement, aspiration and achievement – the heart of our success. We are a leading independent day and boarding school for girls, part of The Girls' Day School Trust. From our 'outstanding' Ofsted rated Nursery; to a revitalised Junior School; exceptionally high-achieving Senior School and dynamic Sixth Form College, the RHS journey is seamless, with four life-enhancing experiences along the way. Results: A level well over 50% A*/A; 84% A*/B IB Exceptionally high average 40 pt score, 55% gain 40 pts or more, way over IB global average score of 30. 100% Oxbridge application success. Overall, 85% are off to their chosen university. GCSE 91.7% A*–B Over 30 girls achieved 10 or more A*/A grades.

The Royal Hospital School, Suffolk, England

Co-ed, Boarding and Day, 11–18

Headmaster Mr J A Lockwood
Holbrook
Ipswich
Suffolk
England
IP9 2RX
T: 01473 326210
E: admissions@royalhospitalschool.org
W: www.royalhospitalschool.org

Age range 11–18; Entry at 11+ (Year 7),
    13+ (Year 9) or 16+ (Sixth Form)
No of pupils 710; Girls 290; Boys 420
Religious denomination Christian
Founded 1712
Member of AGBIS, BSA, HMC, ISA, ISBA
Fees £12,354–£25,437

Set in 200 acres of Suffolk countryside, the Royal Hospital School offers exceptional academic, pastoral and extra-curricular provision. With excellent resources and a curriculum that combines the finest of academic traditions with the latest technologies, pupils are encouraged to develop a love of learning, to aim high and achieve their personal best. The School has a proud reputation for musical excellence and the choir and band play regularly at prestigious venues in the UK and abroad. Fitness and well-being are promoted through the enjoyment of a wide range of sports, from traditional team games to more specialist pursuits such as Olympic pathway sailing tuition and equestrianism. Most importantly, every pupil is encouraged to discover new passions and develop important values that will last a lifetime.

The Royal Masonic School
for Girls, Hertfordshire, England

Girls, Day and Boarding, 11–18

THE ROYAL MASONIC SCHOOL
FOR GIRLS

AT RICKMANSWORTH PARK SINCE 1934

The Headmistress Mrs D Rose
Rickmansworth Park
Rickmansworth
Hertfordshire
England
WD3 4HF
T: 01923 773168
E: enquiries@royalmasonic.herts.sch.uk
W: www.royalmasonic.herts.sch.uk

Age range 11–18
No of pupils 640; Girls 640
Religious denomination
Non-Denominational
Founded 1788
Member of BSA, GSA, ISBA
Fees £14,070–£25,750

Situated in over 150 acres of Hertfordshire parkland just 30 minutes by train from Central London, RMS boasts a long and unique history combined with impressive modern facilities and innovative teaching, to create an outstanding environment in which to learn and grow. RMS offers an exceptionally wide ranging curriculum in a supportive and friendly environment, where the highest standards prevail. Boarders are cared for in well-appointed and spacious houses, with experienced, caring residential staff. In recent OFSTED and ISI inspections RMS was judged as outstanding in both its boarding provision and in all aspects of education, with the girls' academic progress rated as 'exceptional'. Admission is by the school's own entrance examination and interview, and a range of scholarships are available.

SEAFORD
COLLEGE

Seaford College, West Sussex, England

Co-ed, Day and Boarding, 13–18

Headmaster Mr J Green
Lavington Park
Petworth
West Sussex
England
GU28 0NB
T: 01798 867392
E: info@seaford.org
W: www.seaford.org

Age range 13–18
No of pupils 457; Girls 125; Boys 332
Religious denomination Church of
  England
Founded 1884
Member of HMC, SHMIS
Fees £17,850–£27,900

Seaford College is a coeducational independent day and boarding school for pupils aged 7 to 18, situated amid 400 acres of picturesque parkland in West Sussex. The college, with its excellent amenities and outstanding panoramic views, offers an inspirational environment that nurtures academic excellence, sporting success and creative talent. The college uses its resources to provide and enhance educational, cultural, spiritual and social opportunities so that students leave school as confident, articulate and well-rounded individuals. Seaford College offers outstanding sports facilities, including an all-weather water-based Astroturf hockey pitch, golf course and driving range. Students regularly play at county level. Pupils in the Preparatory School at Seaford College share the superb facilities with the Senior School and enjoy a seamless education from 7 to 18.

St Albans School, Hertfordshire, England

Boys, Day only, 11–18

ST ALBANS SCHOOL

The Headmaster Mr Andrew Grant	**Age range** 11–18; Co-ed VIth Form
Abbey Gateway	**No of pupils** 828; Girls 70; Boys 758
St Albans	**Religious denomination**
Hertfordshire	Non-Denominational
England	**Founded** 948
AL3 4HB	**Member of** AGBIS, HMC, ISBA
T: 01727 855521	**Fees** £14,733
E: hm@st-albans-school.org.uk	
W: www.st-albans.herts.sch.uk	

St Albans is a day school for academically able boys aged 11–18 and girls aged 16–18. Founded in 948, its atmosphere and ethos derive from its long tradition and its geographical position near the historic centre of St Albans, in close proximity to the Abbey and overlooking the remains of Roman Verulamium. Whilst maintaining very high standards of academic achievement, it offers wide opportunities for development in other fields: the School's sporting record is exceptional and Drama and Music are strengths, with a distinguished tradition in choral music. Emphasis is laid on the use of individual talents in the service of the community, through the Duke of Edinburgh's Scheme and such activities as Community Service; the Partnership Scheme with local primary schools and the flourishing CCF.

St Benedict's School, London, England

Co-ed, Day only, 11–18

Headmaster Mr Chris Cleugh
54 Eaton Rise, Ealing
London
England
W5 2ES
T: 020 8862 2000
E: enquiries@stbenedicts.org.uk
W: www.stbenedicts.org.uk

Age range 11–18
No of pupils 1090; Girls 318; Boys 772
Religious denomination Roman Catholic
Founded 1902
Member of HMC
Fees £10,560–£12,720

St Benedict's is a co-educational school with a proud academic record. Our Mission of 'Teaching a way of living' is at the core of the holistic Catholic education that is provided to boys and girls throughout the School from Nursery through to Sixth Form. There has been huge recent investment in buildings and facilities, including the award winning £6.2 million Cloisters complex. St Benedict's is renowned for its sporting tradition. Whilst promoting the highest sporting aspirations, the school is committed to sport for all. A wide range of extra-curricular activities is offered including music, drama and opportunities for Christian service. St Benedict's School is unique. Come and visit and see what we have to offer. You can be sure of a warm Benedictine welcome.

St Edmund's College,

Hertfordshire, England

Co-ed, Day and Boarding, 11–18

ST EDMUND'S COLLEGE & PREP SCHOOL

Head Mr P Durán
Old Hall Green
Ware
Hertfordshire
England
SG11 1DS
T: 01920 824247
E: admissions@stedmundscollege.org
W: www.stedmundscollege.org

Age range 11–18
No of pupils 613; Girls 281; Boys 332
Religious denomination Roman Catholic
Founded 1568
Member of AGBIS, BSA, HMC, ISBA
Fees £14,340–£25,989

St Edmund's College, England's oldest Catholic school, is an Independent day and boarding, co-educational Catholic School for boys and girls aged 11–18. St Edmund's College offers an education that challenges and stimulates, developing the whole person in the intellectual, physical, emotional and spiritual areas of life; the richness of our extra-curricular provision and our high-academic standards are testament to the College's success and popularity. Located in rural Hertfordshire, only 40 minutes to London by train, St Edmund's has outstanding transport links and makes full use of the excellent facilities on its 450-acre site including flood-lit astro turf pitches and indoor swimming pool. Scholarships are available at 7+, 11+, 13+ and 16+. St Edmund's welcomes students from all faiths who support our ethos.

St Edward's School, Oxfordshire, England

Co-ed, Boarding and Day, 13–18

ST. EDWARD'S
OXFORD

Warden Mr Stephen Jones
Woodstock Road
Oxford
Oxfordshire
England
OX2 7NN
T: 01865 319200
E: registrar@stedwardsoxford.org
W: www.stedwardsoxford.org

Age range 13–18
No of pupils 670; Girls 270; Boys 400
Religious denomination Church of
    England
Founded 1863
Member of BSA, HMC, IB, ISA, ISBA
Fees £25,671–£32,082

St Edward's is, for a boarding school, a rare and unexpected combination: a sprawling 100-acre estate, complete with grand Quad, over 20 pitches, wide open spaces and riverside boathouse – all a 5-minute cycle ride from the heart of a vibrant international city. Daily interaction with the city of Oxford and the world beyond our perimeter keeps the School atmosphere fresh, and our pupils' feet firmly on the ground. Above all else, St Edward's values a balanced approach to learning and life. We are proud of not being an academic hot-house, and rather than simply recruiting bright students and leading them gently towards exam success, we invest a great deal in each and every child throughout their School career. St Edward's offers a highly-regarded sporting, cultural and extra-curricular programme: our nationally-important public arts centre brings groundbreaking performance and artistic talent right into the heart of School life, whilst our strong sporting tradition allows pupils with potential to become elite sportsmen and women, with growing numbers reaching county and national levels in rugby, hockey, rowing and cricket.

ST HELEN &
ST KATHARINE

St Helen & St Katharine, Oxfordshire, England

Girls, Day only, 11–18

Headmistress Miss R Edbrooke
Faringdon Road
Abingdon
Oxfordshire
England
OX14 1BE
T: 01235 520173
E: admission@shsk.org.uk
W: www.shsk.org.uk

Age range 11–18
No of pupils 700; Girls 700
Religious denomination Church of
England
Founded 1903
Member of AGBIS, GSA, ISBA
Fees £13,020

Founded in 1903, St Helen and St Katharine is an independent day school for girls. 700 pupils, aged 9 to 18, study in a campus of beautiful Victorian and modern buildings, set in 22 acres. St Helen's is a school for bright girls with enquiring minds. Academic results consistently place us amongst the top schools in the country enabling leavers to secure places on their chosen courses at top universities. Our curriculum offers a broad range of subjects: separate sciences, modern and classical languages and the expressive arts. Stimulating and challenging teaching reaches beyond the syllabus, enabling pupils to become effective, enquiring learners. Life beyond the classroom is full and it is this combination which embodies the ethos of the School. Close links with Abingdon School adds a co-educational dimension, with some joint sixth form teaching and collaboration in other activities. Scholarships are available and bursaries of up to 100% of school fees.

St Leonards-Mayfield School,

East Sussex, England

Girls, Day and Boarding, 11–18

Mayfield
ST LEONARDS-MAYFIELD SCHOOL

Headmistress Miss A M Beary
The Old Palace, High Street
Mayfield
East Sussex
England
TN20 6PH
T: 01435 874642
E: admissions@mayfieldgirls.org
W: www.mayfieldgirls.org

Age range 11–18
No of pupils 380; Girls 380
Religious denomination Roman Catholic
Founded 1872
Member of BSA, CIS, GSA

One of the top 10% of independent schools in the UK when measured for delivering a value-added education, and judged 'excellent' across all areas by the Independent Schools Inspectorate in Autumn 2012, St Leonards-Mayfield focuses on enabling all its students to realise their full potential. We assist them to develop their existing talents and discover new ones across a broad curriculum enriched by a wide range of extra-curricular opportunities. Each girl is encouraged to set herself academic goals and is then supported to find the confidence, determination and love of learning to achieve them. Set in the heart of the Sussex countryside, the School provides a caring and supportive community in which girls can flourish and move on successfully to the demands of university and working life.

St Mary's School, Ascot, Berkshire, England

Girls, Boarding and Day, 11–18

Headmistress Mrs Mary Breen
St Mary's Road
Ascot
Berkshire
England
SL5 9JF
T: 01344 296600
E: admissions@st-marys-ascot.co.uk
W: www.st-marys-ascot.co.uk

Age range 11–18; Boarders from 11
No of pupils 382; Girls 382
Religious denomination Roman Catholic
Founded 1885
Member of BSA, GSA
Fees £21,510–£30,240

St Mary's School Ascot is a Roman Catholic boarding school for girls aged 11–18 years. Entry at 11+, 13+ and 16+ is subject to the school's own entry procedure. Facilities are excellent, as is our record in public examinations. We are a friendly, stable and caring community, proud of our academic, sporting and musical achievements and dedicated to bringing out the full potential of each of our pupils. We are committed to full boarding, with spaces for a few day pupils living nearby. We offer a stimulating range of extra-curricular activities which take place in the evenings and throughout the weekend.

St Mary's School, Shaftesbury, Dorset, England

Girls, Boarding and Day, 11–18

Head Mr R James
Shaftesbury
Dorset
England
SP7 9LP
T: 01747 854005
E: admissions@st-marys-shaftesbury.
co.uk
W: www.st-marys-shaftesbury.co.uk

Age range 11–18
No of pupils 320; Girls 320
Religious denomination Roman Catholic
Founded 1940
Member of AGBIS, BSA, GSA
Fees £15,885–£25,998

St Mary's offers an inspiring environment in which girls thrive academically and socially. The pastoral care is outstanding and the friendly atmosphere and warm welcome adds to the community feel of the school. Whilst being forward thinking in approach, there is a strong commitment to traditional values with every girl inspired to reach her potential and achieve a fulfilling and all round education. All talents are nurtured and girls leave as happy, self-confident and successful individuals. At A level 94% of leavers (2012) gained places at Russell Group universities. Girls are given every opportunity to develop new skills and take on new challenges in clubs, societies and weekend activities. Sport, music, art and drama are all flourishing.

STONYHURST

Stonyhurst College, Lancashire, England

Co-ed, Boarding and Day, 13–18

Headmaster Mr A R Johnson
Stonyhurst
Clitheroe
Lancashire
England
BB7 9PZ
T: 01254 827073/093
E: admissions@stonyhurst.ac.uk
W: www.stonyhurst.ac.uk

Age range 13–18
No of pupils 470; Girls 187; Boys 283
Religious denomination Roman Catholic
Founded 1593
Member of AGBIS, BSA, HMC, IB, ISA,
ISBA
Fees £16,392–£29,439

Stonyhurst is set in a magnificent grade I listed building in a beautiful setting. We achieve high academic results, have exceptional pastoral care, and offer an enormous range of extra-curricular opportunities, excelling in sport, the arts and in outward-bound activities. The pupils in our care are given the individual support and resources in which to grow intellectually, spiritually and emotionally. Stonyhurst has an outstanding academic record, with many pupils going on to top universities in the UK (including Oxford and Cambridge), Europe and around the world. In the sixth form we offer the International Baccalaureate alongside A levels. Stonyhurst is a 7-day-a-week boarding school with a busy weekend programme: boarders thrive in a happy, well-ordered environment, in high-quality accommodation.

STRATHALLAN
Opportunities *for all* to excel

Strathallan School, Perthshire, Scotland

Co-ed, Boarding and Day, 13–18

Headmaster Mr B K Thompson
Forgandenny
Perth
Perthshire
Scotland
PH2 9EG
T: +44 1738 812546
E: admissions@strathallan.co.uk
W: www.strathallan.co.uk

Age range 13–18
No of pupils 562; Girls 249; Boys 313
Religious denomination
   Non-Denominational
Founded 1913
Member of BSA, HMC, ISA, ISBA, SCIS
Fees £12,132–£27,249

'Life is wonderful at Strathallan, and I have made so many friends. Most of the pupils board so it makes a huge difference to the atmosphere of the School and there is never a dull moment as we have so much to do academically as well as sport, music and activities.'

Holding an international reputation within its own portfolio of achievements, we need little introduction to those seeking a high-quality boarding establishment for their children. With a nurturing environment and support from teachers passionate about their subjects we achieved 82% A*/B at A level. Set in glorious countryside with 153 acres we offer a safe and secure environment for children to grow and develop and yet within 40 minutes from international airports making the travel from London Heathrow less than 2 hours. Come and see us and experience what we have to offer.

Surbiton High School, Surrey, England

Girls, Day only, 11–18

Principal Miss A Haydon
13–15 Surbiton Crescent
Kingston Upon Thames
Surrey
England
KT1 2JT
T: 020 8546 5245
E: admissions@surbitonhigh.com
W: www.surbitonhigh.com

Age range 11–18
No of pupils 1265; Girls 1265
Religious denomination Christian
Founded 1884
Member of HMC
Fees £8,600–£14,200

An independent academic HMC School for girls aged 4–18 and boys aged 4–11 years, which caters for the individual. Surbiton High School is an enthusiastic, lively and successful community with a long tradition of excellence in pastoral care, where each pupil is valued and inspired to be the best they can be. All are challenged to aim high, think creatively and develop enquiring, critical minds. Ann Haydon, Principal since 2008, is committed to bringing out the 'best in everyone'. The school has been redeveloped to provide purpose built classrooms, Science and Language laboratories, an open plan Art Studio, a separate Sixth Form Centre and extensive sports grounds including a pavilion, hockey pitches, and tennis and netball courts. The school is well served by school buses and public transport.

LOYAUTE ME OBLIGE

Thetford Grammar School, Norfolk, England

Co-ed, Day only, 11–18

Head Mr G J Price
24 Bridge Street
Thetford
Norfolk
England
IP24 3AF
T: 01842 752840
E: hmsec@thetgram.norfolk.sch.uk
W: www.thetgram.norfolk.sch.uk

Age range 11–18
No of pupils 314; Girls 146; Boys 168
Religious denomination
    Non-Denominational
Founded 1114
Member of AGBIS, ISBA
Fees £9,616–£11,630

Thetford Grammar School is a small, friendly and family based community that is one of East Anglia's highest achieving co-educational day schools. We place great emphasis on providing a supportive environment, where pupils take responsibility for themselves and each other. Academic success is at the heart of our activities but as important is the development of the whole person. We encourage creativity through Art, Music, Drama, Sport and indeed in every classroom. The traditions of hard work and extra-curricular activity are blended with an awareness of the need to produce rounded individuals, sensitive to others and fully equipped to meet the challenges of a modern technological society. Our long history reaches right back into the Middle Ages but our modern outlook reaches well into the future.

Tormead School, Surrey, England

Girls, Day only, 11–18

Headmistress Mrs C Foord
27 Cranley Road
Guildford, Surrey
England
GU1 2JD
T: 01483 575101
E: registrar@tormeadschool.org.uk
W: www.tormeadschool.org.uk

Age range 11–18
No of pupils 550; Girls 550
Religious denomination
   Inter-Denominational
Founded 1905
Member of GSA
Fees £6,720–£13,140

At Tormead we believe in doing ordinary things extraordinarily well. We encourage each girl to find her own ways to excel. We have high academic expectations, whilst also giving the pastoral care and support every girl needs to achieve. The curriculum offers breadth and challenge and ensures each girl gains a firm foundation to her education, providing the core skills and knowledge that she will need in the future. We offer the opportunity to shoulder responsibility, take risks, inspire and lead others. A great preparation for life beyond school. We value the girls record of exam success (on average 10% each year are offered places at Oxbridge) as much as we value their effort and achievements outside the classroom, in sport, the performing arts, design and their many contributions to the wider community.

Tring Park School for the Performing Arts, Hertfordshire, England

Co-ed, Boarding and Day, 11–19

The Principal Mr S Anderson
Tring Park
Tring
Hertfordshire
England
HP23 5LX
T: 01442 824255
E: info@tringpark.com
W: www.tringpark.com

Age range 11–19
No of pupils 295; Girls 200; Boys 95
Religious denomination Christian
Founded 1919
Member of BSA, ISA, SHMIS
Fees £18,510–£30,090

Tring Park stands at the forefront of artistic specialist education in the UK. It offers a unique opportunity for young people who show an outstanding talent for the performing arts and aspire to an associated career, while still recognising the benefits of a fine academic education. Tring Park provides a unique community for talented young people, regardless of means or background, who have a passion for Dance, Drama, Musical Theatre or Music. Tring Park nurtures creativity and aims for excellence at all times. Tring Park is dedicated to the provision of a challenging and diverse learning experience within a supportive environment. Government scholarships are available for Dance and limited school scholarships and bursaries available for Musical Theatre or Drama. The Prep Department offers an enriched, integrated curriculum with a unique balance between academic and vocational studies to suit the 'budding' performer with specialist teachers in Dance, Drama and Music.

Tudor Hall School, Oxfordshire, England

Girls, Boarding and Day, 11–18

Headmistress Miss W Griffiths
Wykham Lane Park
Banbury
Oxfordshire
England
OX16 9UR
T: 01295 263434
E: admissions@tudorhallschool.com
W: www.tudorhallschool.com

Age range 11–18
No of pupils 332; Girls 332
Religious denomination
  Church of England
Founded 1850
Member of BSA, GSA, ISA
Fees £17,862–£28,035

Tudor Hall School is unique in so many ways. It is a small, vibrant, full boarding and day school for girls aged 11 to 18 which definitely 'punches above its weight'. The academic results are excellent, produced by young women who have been selected for places at the school not just on their academic ability but also their personal strengths. The girls are not of one type and this creates a community where everybody recognises its members as individuals and celebrates this. Staff work with pupils to ensure that each one is encouraged and supported to do her best. The girls are ambitious and determined to make the most of the many opportunities in school and beyond.

Uppingham School, Rutland, England

Co-ed, Boarding and Day, 13–18

Headmaster Mr R S Harman
High Street West, Uppingham
Oakham
Rutland
England
LE15 9QE
T: 01572 822216
E: admissions@uppingham.co.uk
W: www.uppingham.co.uk

Age range 13–18
No of pupils 780; Girls 345; Boys 435
Religious denomination Church of
England
Founded 1584
Member of BSA, HMC, ISBA
Fees £15,690–£22,098

Uppingham is one of the UK's leading boarding schools for boys and girls aged 13–18, drawing around 780 pupils from all over the country and abroad. Located in the rural setting of a small market town in Rutland, Uppingham's distinctive architecture testifies a history that began in 1584. Whilst the School is noted for its strong commitment to all round education, its superb pastoral care and magnificent facilities, the pupils' academic studies are the priority. The outstanding facilities attract high-quality staff who are keen to be involved with ambitious and purposeful pupils in programmes that extend into busy weekends that regularly include sport and cultural events. Looking forward, a new Science Centre is currently under construction, due to open in 2014 and the ethos of the new building will aim to open up Science to all. If pupils are willing to be helped and guided there is virtually nothing they cannot achieve at Uppingham.

Wellington College, Berkshire, England

Co-ed, Boarding and Day, 13–18

WELLINGTON
COLLEGE

Master Dr A F Seldon
Duke's Ride
Crowthorne
Berkshire
England
RG45 7PU
T: 01344 444013
E: admissions@wellingtoncollege.org.uk
W: www.wellingtoncollege.org.uk

Age range 13–18
No of pupils 1050; Girls 404; Boys 646
Religious denomination Church of
England
Founded 1853
Member of AGBIS, BSA, HMC, IB, ISBA
Fees £24,330–£32,940

Established in 1851 as the memorial to the Duke of Wellington, Wellington is one of the world's great schools. It is set in 400 acres of beautiful parkland and iconic buildings, and has offered an outstanding education to boys (and now girls) for over 150 years. As the UK's top co-ed full boarding school, it achieves outstanding academic results. But it offers more than exam success: it offers an experience which is both energising and inspirational, creatively fusing history and tradition with a 21st-century commitment to innovation and globalism. Wellingtonians study a national and international curriculum of IGCSEs, GCSEs, A levels and the IB and they go on to the world's best universities. The school's unique 'eight aptitude' approach and its ambitious and successful extra-curricular programme: sports, arts, service, well-being and leadership all help to develop the talents of all and to ensure that each Wellingtonian flourishes and becomes the best that they can be.

Westminster, London, England

Co-ed, Boarding and Day, 13–18

Head Master Dr Stephen Spurr
Little Dean's Yard
Westminster
London
England
SW1P 3PF
T: 020 7963 1003
E: registrar@westminster.org.uk
W: www.westminster.org.uk

Age range 13–18
No of pupils 744; Girls 132; Boys 612
Religious denomination
  Church of England
Founded 1560
Member of BSA, HMC
Fees £21,708–£31,350

Situated next to the Houses of Parliament and Westminster Abbey, Westminster is one of the country's leading academic schools. Every year between 40 and 45% of leavers go to Oxford or Cambridge and an increasing number go to universities in the USA. In 2012 53% of A level grades were A* or Pre-U equivalent. Music, art, drama and sport are all important. The games fields and indoor sports centre are a 10 minute walk from the school. The Sixth Form has been co-ed since 1973. Entry at 16+ is by competitive examination and candidates register online. At 13+ the Common Entrance pass mark is 70% and there is also a scholarship examination. A Queen's Scholarship is worth 50% of the boarding fee. Boys entering the school at 13+ are pre-tested while they are in Year 6.

Whitgift School, Surrey, England

Boys, Day only, 11–18

Headmaster Dr C A Barnett
Haling Park
South Croydon
Surrey
England
CR2 6YT
T: 020 8688 9222
E: admissions@whitgift.co.uk
W: www.whitgift.co.uk

Age range 11–18; Boarding from 13–18
No of pupils 1420; Boys 1420
Religious denomination
  Inter-Denominational
Founded 1596
Member of AGBIS, BSA, HMC, IB, IBSCA, ISBA
Fees £15,291–£31,500

WHITGIFT SCHOOL – an outstanding education for over 400 years – now with boarding places. Whitgift, a leading UK independent boys school, offers boarding, from September 2013, for boys aged 13–18. We have an unsurpassed curriculum with excellent academic results, unrivalled sporting success with 63 national titles won in the past two years, an extensive Performing Arts programme, and an exciting range of co-curricular activities. The School offers generous scholarships and bursaries. For further details regarding Whitgift Boarding, please contact the admissions office at admissions@whitgift.co.uk, telephone 020 8688 9222.

Withington Girls' School,

Greater Manchester, England

Girls, Day only, 11–18

Headmistress Mrs S E Marks

100 Wellington Road, Fallowfield

Manchester

Greater Manchester

England

M14 6BL

T: 0161 224 1077

E: office@withington.manchester.sch.uk

W: www.withington.manchester.sch.uk

Age range 11–18

No of pupils 650; Girls 650

Religious denomination
　Inter-Denominational

Founded 1890

Member of AGBIS, GSA, ISBA

Fees £8,238–£11,058

Withington's acclaimed careers advice and regionally unrivalled expertise in securing places on competitive courses in highly selective universities – 92% over three years – complement outstanding examination results that consistently place the school near the top of performance league tables. A happy and purposeful atmosphere nurtures independent minds and high aspirations; girls relish an exceptional range of extra-curricular activities from Music and Drama to Sport, Mathematics and Science Olympiads, Model United Nations, travel and Duke of Edinburgh's Award and Young Enterprise Schemes. Pupils come from a wide geographical area and the School community is proud of its multicultural and multi-faith nature and inclusiveness. One-in-six Senior School girls receives means-tested bursary support.

SENIOR SCHOOLS
INDEX OF GEOGRAPHIC REGIONS

The South East

The Abbey School
Berkshire

Ardingly College
West Sussex

Ashford School
Kent

Bedales School
Hampshire

Benenden School
Kent

Box Hill School
Surrey

Bradfield College
Berkshire

Brighton and Hove High School GDST
East Sussex

Brighton College
East Sussex

Caterham School
Surrey

Charterhouse
Surrey

Christ's Hospital
West Sussex

Churchers College Senior School
Hampshire

City of London Freemen's School
Surrey

Claremont Fan Court School
Surrey

Cobham Hall
Kent

Cranleigh School
Surrey

Downe House
Berkshire

Eastbourne College
East Sussex

Epsom College
Surrey

Eton College
Berkshire

Framlingham College
Suffolk

Frensham Heights School
Surrey

Guildford High School
Surrey

Haileybury
Hertfordshire

Heathfield School, Ascot
Berkshire

Hurstpierpoint College
West Sussex

Hurtwood House
Surrey

Kent College Canterbury
Kent

Kent College Pembury
Kent

King Edward VI School
Hampshire

King's Rochester
Kent

The King's School
Kent

Kingston Grammar School
Surrey

Lancing College
West Sussex

Leighton Park School
Berkshire

Lord Wandsworth College
Hampshire

LVS Ascot
Berkshire

Old Palace of John Whitgift School
Surrey

The Oratory School
Berkshire

Our Lady's Abingdon School
Oxfordshire

Padworth College
Berkshire

Pangbourne College
Berkshire

The Portsmouth Grammar School
Hampshire

Prior's Field
Surrey

Queen Anne's School
Berkshire

Reading Blue Coat School
Berkshire

Reed's School
Surrey

Reigate Grammar School, Guildford
Surrey

Roedean School
East Sussex

Royal Grammar School, Guildford
Surrey

The Royal Hospital School
Suffolk

The Royal Masonic School for Girls
Hertfordshire

Royal Russell School
Surrey

Ryde School
Isle of Wight

Seaford College
West Sussex

Sevenoaks School
Kent

Sir William Perkins's School
Surrey

St Albans School
Hertfordshire

St Bede's School
East Sussex

St Edmund's College
Hertfordshire

St Edmund's School Canterbury
Kent

St George's College
Surrey

St Helen & St Katharine
Oxfordshire

St James Independent School for Boys (Senior)
Surrey

St John's School
Surrey

St Leonards-Mayfield School
East Sussex

St Mary's School, Ascot
Berkshire

Stowe School
Buckinghamshire

Trinity School
Surrey

Surbiton High School
Surrey

Wellington College
Berkshire

Sutton High School GDST
Surrey

Winchester College
Hampshire

Sutton Valence School
Kent

Woldingham School
Surrey

Tonbridge School
Kent

Worth School
West Sussex

Tormead School
Surrey

Wycombe Abbey School
Buckinghamshire

The South West and Wales

Badminton School
Bristol

Cheadle Hulme School
Cheshire

Blundell's School
Devon

Christ College
Powys

Bristol Grammar School
Bristol

Clayesmore
Dorset

Bruton School for Girls
Somerset

Clifton College
Bristol

Bryanston School
Dorset

Clifton High School
Bristol

Canford School
Dorset

Dauntsey's School
Wiltshire

Downside School
Somerset

Elizabeth College
Channel Islands

Exeter School
Devon

The Godolphin School
Wiltshire

The Grange School
Cheshire

Haberdashers' Monmouth School For Girls
Monmouthshire

Kelly College
Devon

King Edward's School, Bath
Bath & North East Somerset

King's Bruton
Somerset

King's College
Somerset

The King's School
Cheshire

Kingswood School
Bath & North East Somerset

Llandovery College
Carmarthenshire

Marlborough College
Wiltshire

The Maynard School
Devon

Millfield School
Somerset

Monkton Senior School
Bath & North East Somerset

Monmouth School
Monmouthshire

Plymouth College
Devon

Prior Park College
Bath & North East Somerset

Queen Elizabeth's Hospital
Bristol

Queen's College
Somerset

The Queen's School
Cheshire

Redland High School for Girls
Bristol

The Red Maids' School
Bristol

The Royal High School, Bath
Bath & North East Somerset

Rydal Penrhos School
Conwy

Truro School
Cornwall

Sherborne Girls
Dorset

Victoria College
Channel Islands

St Mary's Calne
Wiltshire

Warminster School
Wiltshire

St Mary's School, Shaftsbury
Dorset

Wellington School
Somerset

Stockport Grammar School
Cheshire

Wells Cathedral School
Somerset

Taunton School Senior
Somerset

London

Alleyn's School
London

Eltham College
London

Bancroft's School
Essex

Forest School
London

City of London School
London

Francis Holland School, Regent's Park NW1
London

City of London School for Girls
London

The Godolphin and Latymer School
London

Colfe's School
London

Hampton School
Middlesex

Dulwich College
London

Harrow School
Middlesex

Heathfield School for Girls
Middlesex

Highgate School
London

James Allen's Girls' School
London

The John Lyon School
Middlesex

King's College School
London

The Lady Eleanor Holles School
Middlesex

Latymer Upper School
London

Merchant Taylors' School
Middlesex

Mill Hill School
London

North London Collegiate
Middlesex

Putney High School GDST
London

South Hampstead High School
London

St Benedict's School
London

St Dunstan's College
London

St Paul's Girls' School
London

St Paul's School
London

University College School
London

Westminster
London

Whitgift School
Surrey

Wimbledon High School GDST
London

The Midlands and the East

Abingdon School
Oxfordshire

Aldenham School
Hertfordshire

Bablake School
West Midlands

Bedford Girls School
Bedfordshire

Bedford Modern School
Bedfordshire

Bedford School
Bedfordshire

Berkhamsted School
Hertfordshire

Bishop's Stortford College
Hertfordshire

Brentwood School
Essex

Bromsgrove School
Worcestershire

Chase Academy
Staffordshire

Cheltenham College
Gloucestershire

Cheltenham Ladies' College
Gloucestershire

Chigwell School
Essex

Culford School
Suffolk

Dean Close School
Gloucestershire

Derby Grammar School
Derbyshire

Derby High School
Derbyshire

d'Overbroeck's College Oxford
Oxfordshire

Edgbaston High School for Girls
West Midlands

Felsted School
Essex

Gresham's School
Norfolk

Haberdashers' Aske's Boys' School
Hertfordshire

Haberdashers' Aske's School for Girls
Hertfordshire

Headington School
Oxfordshire

Hereford Cathedral School
Herefordshire

Immanuel College
Hertfordshire

Ipswich School
Suffolk

Kimbolton School
Cambridgeshire

King Edward VI High School for Girls
West Midlands

King Edward's School
West Midlands

King Henry VIII School
West Midlands

King's Ely
Cambridgeshire

The King's School
Gloucestershire

The King's School
Worcestershire

Leicester Grammar School
Leicestershire

Leicester High School For Girls
Leicestershire

The Leys School
Cambridgeshire

Lichfield Cathedral School
Staffordshire

Lincoln Minster School
Lincolnshire

Loughborough Grammar School
Leicestershire

Magdalen College School
Oxfordshire

Malvern College
Worcestershire

Malvern St James Girls' School
Worcestershire

Moreton Hall School
Shropshire

New Hall School
Essex

Newcastle-under-Lyme School
Staffordshire

Norwich High School for Girls GDST
Norfolk

Norwich School
Norfolk

Nottingham High School
Nottinghamshire

Nottingham High School for Girls GDST
Nottinghamshire

Oakham School
Rutland

Oundle School
Northamptonshire

Oxford High School GDST
Oxfordshire

The Perse School
Cambridgeshire

The Purcell School
Hertfordshire

Queenswood
Hertfordshire

Radley College
Oxfordshire

Rendcomb College
Gloucestershire

Repton School
Derbyshire

RGS Worcester & The Alice Ottley School
Worcestershire

Rugby School
Warwickshire

Shiplake College
Oxfordshire

Shrewsbury High School GDST
Shropshire

Shrewsbury School
Shropshire

Sibford School
Oxfordshire

Solihull School
West Midlands

St Columba's College
Hertfordshire

St Edward's School
Oxfordshire

Stamford High School
Lincolnshire

Stamford School
Lincolnshire

Thetford Grammar School
Norfolk

Tring Park School for the Performing Arts
Hertfordshire

Tudor Hall School
Oxfordshire

Uppingham School
Rutland

Warwick School
Warwickshire

Wisbech Grammar School
Cambridgeshire

Wolverhampton Grammar School
West Midlands

Worksop College
Nottinghamshire

Wycliffe College
Gloucestershire

The North of England

Abbey Gate College
Cheshire

Ampleforth College
North Yorkshire

Arnold School
Lancashire

Birkdale School
South Yorkshire

Birkenhead School
Merseyside

Bolton School (Boys' Division)
Lancashire

Bolton School (Girls' Division)
Lancashire

Bootham School
North Yorkshire

Bradford Grammar School
West Yorkshire

Bury Grammar School Boys
Lancashire

Bury Grammar School Girls
Lancashire

Campbell College
County Antrim

Chetham's School of Music
Greater Manchester

Dame Allan's Boys School
Tyne and Wear

Dame Allan's Girls School
Tyne and Wear

Durham High School for Girls
County Durham

Giggleswick School
North Yorkshire

The Grammar School at Leeds
West Yorkshire

Harrogate Ladies' College
North Yorkshire

Hymers College
East Riding of Yorkshire

Kirkham Grammar School
Lancashire

The Manchester Grammar School
Greater Manchester

Manchester High School for Girls
Greater Manchester

Merchant Taylors' Boys' Schools
Merseyside

Merchant Taylors' Girls' School
Merseyside

Silcoates School
West Yorkshire

Methodist College
County Antrim

St Bede's College
Greater Manchester

Pocklington School
East Riding of Yorkshire

St Bees School
Cumbria

Queen Elizabeth Grammar School
West Yorkshire

St Peter's School
North Yorkshire

Queen Elizabeth's Grammar School
Lancashire

Stonyhurst College
Lancashire

Rossall School
Lancashire

Wakefield Girls' High School
West Yorkshire

Royal Grammar School
Tyne and Wear

Withington Girls' School
Greater Manchester

Sedbergh School
Cumbria

Woodhouse Grove School
West Yorkshire

Sheffield High School GDST
South Yorkshire

Yarm School
Stockton-on-Tees

Scotland

Dollar Academy
Clackmannanshire

George Heriot's School
Lothian

The Edinburgh Academy
Lothian

George Watson's College
Lothian

Fettes College
Lothian

The Glasgow Academy
Glasgow

Glenalmond College
Perth and Kinross

Gordonstoun School
Morayshire

Kilgraston
Perth and Kinross

The Mary Erskine School
Lothian

Merchiston Castle School
Lothian

Morrison's Academy
Perth and Kinross

Robert Gordon's College
Aberdeenshire

St Leonards School
Fife

Stewart's Melville College
Lothian

Strathallan School
Perthshire

"We are glad that we turned to Gabbitas four years ago for guardianship services and advice."

Mr Cherdabayev, Russia

Guardianship

- Appointment of carefully chosen guardian families

- Dedicated staff in London, Japan, China, Russia and Korea who speak a wide range of languages and offer 24/7 support

- Homestay Programmes

- Support Programme for new students — school and university

- University Mentoring Service

- Family Vetting Service for parents & schools

- VIP Service

- Gabbitas School Emergency Service

☎ **+44 (0)20 7734 0161**
@ **guardian@gabbitas.co.uk**
🌐 **www.gabbitas.co.uk**

Gabbitas Education
CONSULTANTS SINCE 1873

The global experts in British independent education

PART 2
PREPARATORY SCHOOLS

200

THE GABBITAS TOP 200 INDEPENDENT PREPARATORY SCHOOLS

The very best prep schools and prep departments in the United Kingdom are presented in this section. By way of introduction we consider some of the different types of prep school and some of the most important features to consider when choosing between them.

One of the biggest decisions parents will ever face is the choice of their child's first school. It begins with the very first step – nursery or kindergarten – and it is, of course, vital that a child settles in happily and enjoys this earliest stage of education because this will lay the foundations and establish the child's relationship with school for the next 15 years!

This crucial first stage can be something of a conundrum. Many nurseries allocate on a first-come, first-served basis and this means getting a child's name down very early indeed – in some cases, soon after birth! Other nurseries and pre-preps have a different approach. Concerned as parents that the children will fit in happily, they wait till much nearer the entrance date and then invite them in. This meeting is not, though, a cause to strike panic into parents' hearts, nor a cue to start teaching two-year-olds the capital cities of Europe. If you can characterise this as an assessment, it must be the gentlest one imaginable.

First steps

Lucie Moore, Headmistress of Cameron House, explains: 'We ask parents to register a year before entry and see the children aged three, when we invite them in during January or February. We have a group of 15 children for a couple of hours in the afternoon and they play games, have a story and a tea party and use construction toys. The feedback we get is very positive – parents say the children had a lovely afternoon and it wasn't at all scary. We all work to make it happy. It's also about finding people who respond to what we do – I can tell on show-rounds who are charmed by the Gruffalo party and who are left stony cold. I'm aiming for a balanced class of boys and girls and ages throughout the year group. It's tricky because they're all adorable and it's a quick snapshot – but we're good at doing it.'

At Durston House, there is a 'taster session' when children entering the reception class have a games lesson, play and perhaps do some music or spend time in a classroom. 'We look at how they play,' says pre-prep Head Hilary Wyatt, 'and communicate with adults and other children, how they sit and hold a pencil. It takes about an hour to assess each child, though for the children they've just come to play and are one of a group. We're not looking for what they know, rather how they respond. We also go and observe them in their own nursery – so we do get to know them very well.'

'There's no point in parents trying to coach them however tempting that may be. We're looking for personality, an interest in life and learning, not what they can record. We notice what their vocabulary is like and whether they can string a sentence together. One child I interviewed while feeding the fish. He wanted to know where they came from, where their eggs came from. He wanted to learn and he got a place.'

At Kensington Prep, Headmistress Prudence Lynch looks for children who will play to their strengths. 'We are a broad based school,' she says, 'but we are very good with able children who want a faster pace. Assessment, though, is an art not a science. It takes about an hour and they are doing the same activities they would do at nursery. We have six or seven at a time and then we spend a little time in another room one to one. It's very unintimidating but we are oversubscribed and you can't take everyone. We're looking for children who will thrive, not just survive, children who are curious and will take intellectual risks. You just see the spark.'

A multitude of choices

Beyond the earliest years, where a nurturing environment is all-important, parents face a number of choices. Many pre-preps lead on naturally to their own preps (aged 7 and upwards) but this is not always an automatic process and parents often consider the later steps their children will be taking when it comes to choosing a prep. One of the biggest questions is whether boarding could be a possibility. Families who are city based with a good selection of schools often go for day schools, even though they may change to boarding for senior school. However, while a few years ago, boarding preps were in decline, they have recently experienced a surge of interest, especially as most now offer weekly boarding which, it can be argued, offers the best of both worlds – all of the possibilities and activities of boarding with normal family life at weekends.

David Gainer, Head of Godstowe Prep in High Wycombe is certainly confident that weekly boarding is growing in popularity – he recently opened a new junior house. 'It's for the 7 to 11 year olds,' he explains, 'and has its own staff, earlier bedtimes, and an even more nurturing environment than the "grown-up" house for the girls in the two top years.' Unusually, Godstowe girls stay until 13 going on to such schools as Benenden and Wycombe Abbey as well as co-ed boarding schools such as Wellington, Arundel and Bradfield – and he sees this as the school's USP – a child-centred prep complete with rolling acres, lots of activities, high-academic standards and plenty of parental contact.

According to Martin Harris of Sandroyd School, this parental contact is what most families want. 'The realisation to a young child that they will see their parents at the end of the week and to a nervous mum that she will see her most prized asset is a happy state of affairs.'

Tom Dawson at Sunningdale in Ascot agrees. 'The idea of having sons and daughters back home at weekends does ease the idea of separation. But many parents recognise the advantages of boarding and its scope for providing an all round education. The academic side is top priority but then they play games every day, at morning break they can run into the woods to build a camp. They are not confined to a small playground shared with the rest of the school. No one who has experienced boarding will forget the camaraderie and banter that goes on in the dorms and it is not simply a cliché to say you make friends for life.'

Given the enormity of the step into boarding, though, many heads, such as Tom Bunbury at Papplewick School in Ascot believe in easing children in gradually. 'We have a daily bus for younger boys – 35 minutes from Chiswick. From eight we offer weekly boarding and it's been growing in popularity since we introduced it a few years ago. It makes sense as many of the public schools we feed, such as Wellington, have weekly boarding themselves and it can offer the best of both worlds. But modern boarding is very different from the way it was even a generation ago and I'm a huge believer that it's not just about a place to sleep at the end of the day. We have extensive activities from magic club to shooting at Bisley and everyone is fully occupied till bedtime. There's a huge sense of community and it's good for families, too.'

Ben Evans of Edge Grove Prep in Hertfordshire encourages parental involvement. 'We like parental contact – you have to listen and be flexible to suit the needs of each particular family and circumstances. We have full boarding but pupils can choose to go home on Friday night or Saturday morning. Once every three weeks we have a Friday off, too, so that they can do things like go to the dentist. For the younger ones we have flexi-boarding. Mostly, the children want to board more and more!'

Edge Grove and most of the other schools mentioned here offer a variety of boarding styles. Many insist in the final year or two on full boarding, albeit with plenty of exeats, as preparation for their senior public schools. All of them take the process of increasing boarding gently and homesickness is rare. At Caldicott School in Slough, all the boys board for the last two years. According to Head Simon Doggart, 'We are mostly a day school up to 11, with many of our pupils taking our bus from Notting Hill. A few board early but most parents want the ethos of a boarding school – they're looking at Eton and Harrow eventually – and convert when they feel ready. We take a wider range of ability and we do well by all of them without pushing and coaching for exams at age seven – and we still get scholarships to the major public schools. We're strong on team ethos, proper meals together with good table manners and conversation. It's traditional and lots of parents want this.'

A special talent?

Some young children display a special talent and, while scholarships are usually available only at secondary level, there are some at a more tender age for the musically talented, especially at choir schools. St Paul's Cathedral Prep was originally established – as with so many choir schools – to educate the choristers. Nowadays, they take many more children who aren't choristers but the school still has the choir at its heart and choristers' tuition fees and music lessons are paid for by the cathedral with bursaries available for the boarding fees. While for most of the 4- to 13-year-olds who are pupils, this is a day school, choristers board so they can work around their choir commitments. St Paul's has 34 choristers and, besides singing in the cathedral, they sing at major public events, at the proms, record CDs and go on tour!

King's School Ely educates the choristers of Ely Cathedral. Up to 22 boy choristers get 50% off their fees and up to 18 girls 33% – none requires means testing. 'It isn't simply a scholarship,' argues Head Sue Freeman. 'We expect an enormous amount back. Boys rehearse every morning before school and choristers sing evensong and services throughout the week and weekend. You're not just talking about talent – they work their socks off! We have bursaries to top up the girls' choral award and for some of the boys, though they can get them, too, from the Choir Schools Association. We also have bursaries for families who fall on hard times while their children are at the school.'

At Wellesley House in Kent, Simon O'Malley, the Head, believes so strongly in bursaries that he has been looking at new ways of funding them. 'We have launched a bursary appeal,' he says, 'to supplement those we already give to pupils who wouldn't be able to afford the fees. The aim is to raise a £500,000 fund for able children and we already raised half of that very quickly in just one year. Then we have sibling discounts, musical awards, two scholarships a year as well as the bursaries.'

Subject matters

Some prep schools, such as Holmwood House, offer academic scholarships from Year 7 and are adept at finding their pupils scholarships in their senior schools. In 2013, for instance, nearly 50% will have a scholarship – academic, music, sport, art or all-rounder – to one of 18 senior schools. One of the keys to this success is specialist teaching from an early age explains Headmaster Alexander Mitchell. 'We introduce specialist teaching from an early age – French, music, swimming, PE and Games in Reception. Then specialist art from Year 2 and science from Year 3. From Year 4, the children are taught in three ability sets by subject specialists across the whole curriculum. This brings passion and understanding in all subjects and our academic monitoring system ensures the whole picture is regularly screened to ensure that progress is consistent.'

Specialist teaching, particularly in such subjects as languages and science starts early in most top preps. Maths, for instance, is a subject that has been the focus of much concern in recent years and is one that leading prep schools take particularly seriously. At Newton Prep, strong foundations are all important as former head Nicholas Allen, explains: 'I've seen maths teaching improve massively over the years. At Newton Prep they teach the basic concepts and give plenty of consolidation, then pupils zoom ahead. Mathletics has been very popular. It's an internet-based maths competition that children enjoy from a very tender age. They do maths and compete with children all over the world. It has an enormous following, children can get points, win things and they progress at their own level.'

Jeremy Edwards, Head of Eaton House, the Manor, believes maths should be fun, too. 'Boys love challenges and we've adapted our curriculum to do more problem solving and the boys enjoy it. The senior schools we feed look for boys who can under-stand mathematical concepts and apply their knowledge. But old-fashioned maths teaching often leaves them with limited understanding. They know to put numbers in columns of units, tens and hundreds but they don't know why, what those columns represent. We've now introduced the Abacus scheme and that has a greater focus on mental maths, understanding number values and concepts. So far it's proving a great success. We apply maths to day-to-day situations like shopping or travelling on the motorway and that helps the boys to understand and enjoy maths. They're secure in their mental maths and that boosts confidence.'

Confidence is key in subjects like maths – and people (including parents who were often not taught well themselves) assume it needs a special kind of mind. 'There's a perception that maths is different from other subjects,' says Dr Emily Macmillan, Head of Maths at the Dragon School in Oxford. 'There's a fear of attempting it and getting it wrong – that it's black and white in a way other subjects aren't. I don't think it is so black and white, though. What we try to do here is show there are grey areas, putting the emphasis on the doing of the maths rather than the answer. It's the process not the answer that's important, knowing *how* to do something. It's important to teach them why we do maths – because it may seem odd to do complex division when you've got a calculator on your phone. But the process is growing your brain and teaching you to be logical. And maths is useful in every part of life. People think it's just punching numbers but it teaches you to spot patterns, to abstract information from problems, draw connections, be critical, apply knowledge. And you can take maths out of the classroom, too. We had a charity event on the playing field where the children had to cover a certain distance between them, so we worked out how many would have to run 50m. It's all about embedding maths into everyday life and making it fun, practical and real.'

It is this commitment to laying down solid foundations for which good preps are renowned. It applies not just to maths but across all subjects and, perhaps even more importantly, it creates the right attitude to learning that should last throughout a child's school career and beyond. So many elements go into the mix that makes a school outstanding – fine teaching, encouragement of individual talent, widening horizons, a safe, nurturing environment and academic achievement. Beechwood Park School's recent 'outstanding in all areas' rating at inspection reflected all of these features. The co-ed prep in Markyate near St Albans was, of course, delighted. Patrick Atkinson, Headmaster, commented, 'My colleagues and I strive for excellence in everything and it is naturally very gratifying that the inspectors concluded our pupils have access to the highest standards of care and provision, as well as fantastic opportunities'. And this is precisely what good preps are all about.

PREPARATORY SCHOOLS LISTING

P = Also in Profiled Schools section
NB   Age ranges are shown for the preparatory school only.
       Age ranges for any senior school departments are not included.

Abberley Hall, Worcestershire **P**
Co-ed, Boarding and Day, 2–13

Aberdour School, Surrey
Co-ed, Day only, 3–13

Aldro School, Surrey
Boys, Boarding and Day, 7–13

All Hallows Preparatory School,
Somerset **P**
Co-ed, Day and Boarding, 3–13

Alleyn's School, London
Co-ed, Day only, 4–11

Ardvreck School, Perth and Kinross
Co-ed, Day and Boarding, 3–13

Arnold House School, London
Boys, Day only, 5–13

Ashdown House School, East Sussex
Co-ed, Boarding only, 8–13

Aysgarth School, North Yorkshire **P**
Boys, Boarding and Day, 3–13

Badminton School, Bristol
Girls, Boarding and Day, 3–11

Beachborough School,
Northamptonshire
Co-ed, Day and Boarding, 2–13

The Beacon School, Buckinghamshire
Boys, Day only, 3–13

Beaudesert Park School,
Gloucestershire
Co-ed, Boarding and Day, 4–13

Bedales Prep School, Dunhurst,
Hampshire
Co-ed, Boarding and Day, 8–13

Bedford Girls School, Bedfordshire
Girls, Day and Boarding, 3–13

Bedford Modern School,
Bedfordshire
Co-ed, Day only, 7–11

Bedford Preparatory School,
Bedfordshire
Boys, Boarding and Day, 7–13

Beechwood Park School,
Hertfordshire
Co-ed, Day and Boarding, 3–13

Beeston Hall School, Norfolk
Co-ed, Boarding and Day, 7–13

Belhaven Hill, Lothian
Co-ed, Boarding and Day, 7–13

Berkhamsted School, Hertfordshire
Co-ed, Day only, 3–11

Bilton Grange, Warwickshire Ⓟ
Co-ed, Day and Boarding, 4–13

Birchfield School, West Midlands
Co-ed, Day and Boarding, 4–13

**Bishop's Stortford College Junior
School**, Hertfordshire
Co-ed, Boarding and Day, 4–13

Blundell's Preparatory School,
Devon
Co-ed, Day only, 3–11

Brabyns School, Cheshire
Co-ed, Day only, 2–11

Brambletye, West Sussex
Co-ed, Boarding and Day, 3–13

Brighton College Prep School,
East Sussex
Co-ed, Day only, 8–13

Bromsgrove Preparatory School,
Worcestershire
Co-ed, Boarding and Day, 7–13

**Bute House Preparatory School for
Girls**, London
Girls, Day only, 4–11

Caldicott School, Buckinghamshire
Boys, Boarding and Day, 7–13

Cameron House School, London Ⓟ
Co-ed, Day only, 4–11

Cargilfield, Lothian
Co-ed, Boarding and Day, 3–13

Chafyn Grove School, Wiltshire
Co-ed, Boarding and Day, 3–13

Cheam School, Berkshire Ⓟ
Co-ed, Day and Boarding, 3–13

Cheltenham College Junior School,
Gloucestershire
Co-ed, Boarding and Day, 3–13

Christ Church Cathedral School,
Oxfordshire
Boys, Day only, 3–13

Claremont Fan Court School, Surrey
Co-ed, Day only, 5–11

Clayesmore Preparatory School,
Dorset
Co-ed, Boarding and Day, 3–13

Clifton College Preparatory School,
Bristol ⓟ
Co-ed, Boarding and Day, 8–13

Colet Court, London
Boys, Day only, 7–13

Copthorne Prep School, West
Sussex
Co-ed, Day and Boarding, 2–13

Cottesmore School, West Sussex
Co-ed, Day and Boarding, 7–13

Craigclowan Preparatory School,
Perth and Kinross
Co-ed, Day only, 3–13

Cranleigh Preparatory School,
Surrey
Co-ed, Boarding and Day, 7–13

Cranmore School, Surrey
Boys, Day only, 3–13

Cumnor House School, Surrey
Boys, Day only, 4–13

Danes Hill School, Surrey ⓟ
Co-ed, Day only, 3–13

Daneshill School, Hampshire
Co-ed, Day only, 2–13

Davenies School, Buckinghamshire
Boys, Day only, 4–13

Dean Close Preparatory School,
Gloucestershire
Co-ed, Boarding and Day, 3–13

Derwent Lodge School for Girls,
Kent
Girls, Day only, 7–11

Devonshire House School, ⓟ
London
Co-ed, Day only, 2–13

The Downs School, Bristol
Co-ed, Day and Boarding, 4–13

The Downs, Malvern, Worcestershire
Co-ed, Boarding and Day, 3–13

Downsend School, Surrey
Co-ed, Day only, 2–13

Dragon School, Oxfordshire
Co-ed, Boarding and Day, 4–13

**Dulwich College Preparatory
School**, London
Boys, Day and Boarding, 3–13

Durston House, London
Boys, Day only, 4–13

Eagle House School, Berkshire (P)
Co-ed, Day and Boarding, 3–13

Eaton House The Manor Girls' School, London
Girls, Day only, 4–11

Edge Grove, Hertfordshire (P)
Co-ed, Day and Boarding, 3–13

Edgeborough, Surrey
Co-ed, Day and Boarding, 2–13

The Elms, Worcestershire
Co-ed, Boarding and Day, 3–13

Elstree School, Berkshire
Boys, Boarding and Day, 3–13

Exeter Cathedral School, Devon
Co-ed, Day and Boarding, 3–13

Farleigh School, Hampshire
Co-ed, Boarding and Day, 3–13

Fettes College, Lothian
Co-ed, Boarding and Day, 4–11

Foremarke Hall, Derbyshire
Co-ed, Day and Boarding, 3–13

Forres Sandle Manor, Hampshire (P)
Co-ed, Boarding and Day, 3–13

The Froebelian School, West Yorkshire
Co-ed, Day only, 3–11

Fulham Prep School, London (P)
Co-ed, Day only, 4–13

Garden House School, London
Co-ed, Day only, 3–11

Gayhurst School, Buckinghamshire (P)
Co-ed, Day only, 3–13

Glendower Preparatory School, London
Girls, Day only, 4–11

Godstowe Preparatory School, Buckinghamshire (P)
Girls, Day and Boarding, 3–13

Gresham's Prep School, Norfolk
Co-ed, Day and Boarding, 8–13

Grosvenor School, Nottinghamshire
Co-ed, Day only, 1–13

Haberdashers' Aske's Boys' School, Herfordshire
Boys, Day only, 5–11

Hall Grove School, Surrey
Co-ed, Day and Boarding, 4–13

The Hall School, London
Boys, Day only, 4–13

Hatherop Castle School, Gloucestershire
Co-ed, Boarding and Day, 2–13

Hawkesdown House School, (P)
London
Boys, Day only, 3–8

The Hawthorns School, Surrey
Co-ed, Day only, 2–13

Hazlegrove Preparatory School,
Somerset (P)
Co-ed, Day and Boarding, 2–13

Headington School, Oxfordshire
Girls, Day and Boarding, 3–11

Heywood Preparatory School,
Wiltshire
Co-ed, Day only, 2–11

Highfield Preparatory School, North
Yorkshire
Co-ed, Day and Boarding, 4–11

Highfield School, Hampshire
Co-ed, Boarding and Day, 8–13

Highgate School, London
Co-ed, Day only, 3–7

Hilden Grange School, Kent
Co-ed, Day only, 3–13

Hilden Oaks School, Kent
Co-ed, Day only, 3–6

**Hill House International Junior
School,** London
Co-ed, Day only, 4–13

Holmewood House, Kent (P)
Co-ed, Day and Boarding, 3–13

**Holmwood House Preparatory
School,** Essex (P)
Co-ed, Day and Boarding, 4–13

Hornsby House School, London
Co-ed, Day only, 4–11

Horris Hill School, Berkshire
Boys, Boarding and Day, 7–13

James Allen's Preparatory School,
London
Co-ed, Day only, 4–11

Junior King's Canterbury, Kent
Co-ed, Day and Boarding, 3–13

Kensington Prep School, London
Girls, Day only, 4–11

Kew Green Preparatory School,
Surrey
Co-ed, Day only, 4–11

Kilgraston, Perth and Kinross
Girls, Boarding and Day, 8–13

King's College Junior School,
London
Boys, Day only, 7–13

King's College School,
Cambridgeshire
Co-ed, Day and Boarding, 4–13

King's Hall, Somerset
Co-ed, Boarding and Day, 3–13

King's House School, Surrey
Boys, Day only, 4–13

King's Preparatory School, Kent
Co-ed, Day and Boarding, 8–13

Kingswood Preparatory School,
Bath & North East Somerset
Co-ed, Day and Boarding, 3–11

Lambrook, Berkshire
Co-ed, Boarding and Day, 3–13

Latymer Prep School, London
Co-ed, Day only, 7–11

Laxton Junior School,
Northamptonshire
Co-ed, Day only, 4–11

Leaden Hall School, Wiltshire
Girls, Day and Boarding, 3–11

Lockers Park, Hertfordshire
Boys, Boarding and Day, 5–13

Ludgrove, Berkshire
Boys, Boarding only, 8–13

Magdalen College Junior School,
Oxfordshire
Boys, Day only, 7–11

Maidwell Hall School,
Northamptonshire
Co-ed, Boarding and Day, 7–13

Malsis School, North Yorkshire
Co-ed, Boarding and Day, 4–13

The Manor Preparatory School,
Oxfordshire
Co-ed, Day only, 2–11

Marlborough House School, Kent
Co-ed, Day and Boarding, 3–13

Millfield Prep School, Somerset ⓟ
Co-ed, Day and Boarding, 2–13

Monkton Prep, Bath & North East
Somerset
Co-ed, Day and Boarding, 2–13

Moor Park School, Shropshire
Co-ed, Boarding and Day, 3–13

Moreton Hall Preparatory School,
Suffolk
Co-ed, Boarding and Day, 2–13

Moulsford Preparatory School,
Oxfordshire
Boys, Boarding and Day, 4–13

Mount House School, Devon
Co-ed, Boarding and Day, 3–13

New College School, Oxfordshire
Boys, Day only, 4–13

New Hall Preparatory School, Essex
Co-ed, Boarding and Day, 4–11

Newton Prep, London
Co-ed, Day only, 3–13

Northcote Lodge School, London
Boys, Day only, 8–13

Northwood Preparatory School,
Hertfordshire
Boys, Day only, 4–13

Notre Dame School, Surrey Ⓟ
Girls, Day only, 4–11

Notting Hill Preparatory School,
London
Co-ed, Day only, 4–13

**Nottingham High School for Girls
GDST**, Nottinghamshire
Girls, Day only, 4–13

The Oratory Preparatory School,
Oxfordshire
Co-ed, Day and Boarding, 3–13

Orley Farm School, Middlesex
Co-ed, Day only, 4–13

Orwell Park, Suffolk
Co-ed, Boarding and Day, 3–13

Packwood Haugh School, Shropshire
Co-ed, Boarding and Day, 4–13

Papplewick, Ascot, Berkshire Ⓟ
Boys, Day and Boarding, 6–13

Pembridge Hall, London
Girls, Day only, 4–11

The Perse School, Cambridgeshire
Co-ed, Day only, 2–11

The Pilgrims' School, Hampshire
Boys, Boarding and Day, 7–13

Pinewood School, Wiltshire
Co-ed, Boarding and Day, 3–13

Port Regis Preparatory School,
Dorset
Co-ed, Boarding and Day, 3–13

The Portsmouth Grammar School,
Hampshire
Co-ed, Day only, 2–11

Prestfelde Preparatory School,
Shropshire
Co-ed, Day and Boarding, 3–13

Prior Park Preparatory School,
Wiltshire
Co-ed, Boarding and Day, 3–13

Priory Preparatory School, Surrey
Boys, Day only, 2–13

**Queen's College Junior, Pre-Prep &
Nursery Schools**, Somerset
Co-ed, Day and Boarding, 3–11

Rokeby School, Surrey
Boys, Day only, 4–13

Rose Hill School, Kent
Co-ed, Day only, 3–13

S. Anselm's School, Derbyshire
Co-ed, Boarding and Day, 3–13

Saint Ronan's School, Kent
Co-ed, Boarding and Day, 3–13

Sandroyd School, Wiltshire
Co-ed, Boarding and Day, 7–13

Sevenoaks Preparatory School, Kent
Co-ed, Day only, 2–13

Sherborne Preparatory School,
Dorset
Co-ed, Day and Boarding, 3–13

Shrewsbury House School, Surrey
Boys, Day only, 7–13

Solefield School, Kent
Boys, Day only, 4–13

Spratton Hall, Northamptonshire
Co-ed, Day only, 4–13

St Andrew's School, East Sussex
Co-ed, Boarding and Day, 2–13

St Bede's Prep School, East Sussex
Co-ed, Boarding and Day, 2–13

St Christopher's School, London
Girls, Day only, 4–11

St Faith's, Cambridgeshire
Co-ed, Day only, 4–13

St Hugh's School, Oxfordshire
Co-ed, Boarding and Day, 3–13

St John's Beaumont, Berkshire Ⓟ
Boys, Boarding and Day, 3–13

St John's College School,
Cambridgeshire
Co-ed, Day and Boarding, 4–13

St John's Northwood, Middlesex
Boys, Day only, 3–13

St John's-on-the-Hill, Monmouthshire,
Wales
Co-ed, Boarding and Day, 3–13

St Martin's Ampleforth, North
Yorkshire
Co-ed, Boarding and Day, 3–13

St Michael's Preparatory School,
Channel Islands
Co-ed, Day only, 3–13

St Olave's School, Yorkshire
Co-ed, Day and Boarding, 4–11

St Paul's Cathedral School,
London Ⓟ
Co-ed, Day and Boarding, 7–13

St Piran's Preparatory School,
Berkshire
Co-ed, Day only, 3–13

Stamford Junior School, Lincolnshire
Co-ed, Boarding and Day, 2–11

Stonyhurst St Mary's Hall,
Lancashire Ⓟ
Co-ed, Day and Boarding, 3–13

The Study Preparatory School, London
Girls, Day only, 4–11

Summer Fields, Oxfordshire
Boys, Boarding and Day, 7–13

Sunningdale School, Berkshire
Boys, Boarding only, 8–13

Sussex House School, London
Boys, Day only, 8–13

Swanbourne House School, Buckinghamshire
Co-ed, Boarding and Day, 3–13

Terra Nova School, Cheshire
Co-ed, Day and Boarding, 3–13

Tockington Manor School, Bristol
Co-ed, Day and Boarding, 2–14

Twyford School, Hampshire
Co-ed, Day and Boarding, 3–13

Vinehall School, East Sussex
Co-ed, Boarding and Day, 2–13

Walhampton, Hampshire **P**
Co-ed, Boarding and Day, 2–13

Wellesley House School, Kent
Co-ed, Boarding and Day, 7–13

Wellingborough School, Northamptonshire
Co-ed, Day only, 3–11

Wells Cathedral Junior School, Somerset
Co-ed, Boarding and Day, 3–11

West Hill Park School, Hampshire **P**
Co-ed, Day and Boarding, 3–13

Westbourne House School, West Sussex
Co-ed, Boarding and Day, 2–13

Westminster Abbey Choir School, London
Boys, Boarding only, 8–13

Westminster Cathedral Choir School, London
Boys, Boarding and Day, 7–13

Westminster Under School, London
Boys, Day only, 7–13

Wetherby Preparatory School, London
Boys, Day only, 8–13

Wimbledon High School GDST, London
Girls, Day and Boarding, 4–11

Winchester House School, Northamptonshire
Co-ed, Boarding and Day, 3–13

Windlesham House School, West Sussex
Co-ed, Boarding and Day, 4–13

Yardley Court Preparatory School,
Kent
Boys, Day only, 7–13

Yarm Preparatory School, Cleveland
Co-ed, Day only, 4–11

Yateley Manor Preparatory School,
Hampshire
Co-ed, Day only, 3–13

York House School, Hertfordshire
Co-ed, Day only, 3–13

PREPARATORY SCHOOLS PROFILED SCHOOLS

Abberley Hall, Worcestershire, England
Co-ed, Boarding and Day, 2–13

Headmaster Mr John Walker
Abberley Hall, Abberley
Worcester
Worcestershire
England
WR6 6DD
T: 01299 896275
E: john.walker@abberleyhall.co.uk
W: www.abberleyhall.co.uk

Age range 2–13
No of pupils 286; Girls 115; Boys 171
Religious denomination Non-
Denominational
Founded 1878
Member of HMC, IAPS
Fees £4,440–£19,440

Abberley Hall is a co-educational boarding school for 8–13 year olds, and has a number of day pupils (2–13yrs). Abberley prepares pupils for all good public schools. It provides the academic, sporting and social grounding which is the foundation for sustained success. Our aim is to achieve an informal and friendly approach to school life combined with the discipline that enables all pupils to reach their full potential. The facilities are outstanding and include a new science block, art and DT complex, sports hall with indoor cricket nets, Astroturf pitch, tennis courts, indoor swimming pool, riding school, large music suite, theatre, fishing lake and much more. The school owns a chalet in the French Alps. Abberley Hall, Worcestershire, WR6 6DD 01299 896275. Visit our web site on www.abberleyhall.co.uk

All Hallows Preparatory School,
Somerset, England

Co-ed, Day and Boarding, 3–13

ALL HALLOWS
Preparatory School

Headmaster Mr Ian Murphy

Cranmore Hall

Shepton Mallet

Somerset

England

BA4 4SF

T: 01749 881600

E: info@allhallowsschool.co.uk

W: www.allhallowsschool.co.uk

Age range 3–13

No of pupils 284; Girls 150; Boys 134

Religious denomination Roman Catholic

Member of AGBIS, BSA, HMC, IAPS, ISA, NAHT

Fees £2,410–£6,715

All Hallows is a very special place to grow, live and work, a school radiating warmth and vibrancy. At the heart of All Hallows' success is a vision aimed at nurturing each individual and developing the 'whole child' through cutting-edge education and rich and varied experiences, underpinned by the unswerving certainty that Christian values are paramount. This unique school provides a secure and happy environment where children will develop the inner confidence necessary to flourish in a rapidly changing world. Whilst protected and nurtured, the children are also challenged and stretched in order to build their ability to thrive as adults in the future. Rated as 'Outstanding' by Ofsted. Situated in a west-country, rural location in 25 acres surrounded by open countryside and farmland, the school is close to the major cities of Bath, Wells and Bristol.

Aysgarth School, North Yorkshire, England

Boys, Boarding and Day, 3–13

Head Mr C A A Goddard
Aysgarth School, Newton le Willows
Bedale
North Yorkshire
England
DL8 1TF
T: 01677 450240
E: enquiries@aysgarthschool.co.uk
W: www.aysgarthschool.com

Age range 3–13; Girls 3–8
Religious denomination Church of
England
Founded 1877
Member of BSA, IAPS, ISA
Fees £6,970–£20,970

Aysgarth School is one of the UK's leading Prep Schools for boys. It also has a co-ed Nursery and Pre-Prep for children up to 8 years. Aysgarth Prep School offers boys the opportunity to experience a traditional childhood, specifically providing for boys' needs and enthusiasms. As the only all-boys' Prep boarding school in the North of England, we are unique. We hold an unmatched record in the North of sending boys to the most selective schools such as Harrow and Eton. Boys thrive on adventure – seemingly quiet children will do far more than they thought they could when given the opportunity to enjoy a variety of activities as well as challenging classroom assignments, and the more energetic boy will keep focused for longer. Our goal is to find the best in every boy – whether they excel academically, in sport or through creative arts. Between the ages of 8 and 13 years, boys often thrive when they are not with girls, in or out of the classroom. This is not just about adventure as we also seek to develop pupil's thoughtful, sensitive side, encouraging courtesy, kindness and respect for others.

Bilton Grange, Warwickshire, England

Co-ed, Day and Boarding, 4–13

Headmaster Mr A Osiatynski
Rugby Road, Dunchurch
Rugby
Warwickshire
England
CV22 6QU
T: 01788 810217
E: admissions@biltongrange.co.uk
W: www.biltongrange.co.uk

Age range 4–13
No of pupils 321; Girls 124; Boys 197
Religious denomination Church of
England
Founded 1887
Member of BSA, IAPS, ISBA
Fees £8,910–£21,540

Set in 100 acres of Warwickshire parkland, Bilton Grange is one of the UK's leading prep schools, feeding over 30 top independent senior schools. Children are able to enjoy their childhood at Bilton Grange, and achieve cross curricular success without pressure. Confident not arrogant, pupils continue to flourish when they move on to senior school, having been well prepared at Bilton Grange. From the early years in Pre-Prep, to all the challenges of the upper years of Prep School, children benefit from the school's top facilities, small classes taught by specialist teachers, and high levels of pastoral care. Families are warmly encouraged to come and see what a Bilton Grange education is all about by contacting the Registrar, Rebecca Bantoft, on 01788 818249 or rlb@biltongrange.co.uk.

Cameron House School, London, England

Co-ed, Day only, 4–11

The Headmistress Mrs Lucie Moore
4 The Vale, Chelsea
London, England
SW3 6AH
T: 020 7352 4040
E: info@cameronhouseschool.org
W: www.cameronhouseschool.org

Age range 4–11
No of pupils 120; Girls 66; Boys 54
Religious denomination
  Non-Denominational
Founded 1980
Member of CReSTeD, IAPS, NAHT
Fees £15,750

Cameron House is a vibrant school well-known for maintaining high academic standards while encouraging individual creativity. Children leave the school as independent thinkers, brimming with intellectual curiosity. This approach produces an outstanding response in the attitudes of pupils towards learning and towards school life. Both boys and girls are thoroughly prepared for entrance exams and scholarships at 11 for prestigious London day and boarding schools. While emphasis is placed on the core curriculum, the school's teaching goes far beyond. All study a comprehensive range of subjects. French is taught from Reception and music, singing, speech and drama are popular – as is debating. The high staff: pupil ratio allows the dedicated teachers to create a stimulating, tailored learning environment. Interactive Whiteboards in every classroom and a bank of laptops provide access to online learning and each class also has its own library. A varied sports programme gives the children opportunities to take part in lessons, matches and tournaments several times a week. Numerous after school clubs foster interests including: fencing, drama, karate, ballet, orchestra, chess, choir and Latin to name just a few. We encourage all our children to consider and care for others. Staff and pupils have a sense of belonging and purpose, which supports children of all abilities in achieving excellent standards.

Cheam School, Berkshire, England

Co-ed, Day and Boarding, 3–13

Cheam School

Head Master Mr Mark Johnson
Newbury Road, Headley
Thatcham
Berkshire
England
RG19 8LD
T: 01635 268381
E: office@cheamschool.co.uk
W: www.cheamschool.com

Age range 3–13
No of pupils 414; Girls 196; Boys 218
Religious denomination Church of
England
Founded 1645
Member of BSA, HAS, HMC, IAPS, ISA,
ISBA, NAHT, NAIS
Fees £10,260–£24,270

Curriculum: Children are prepared in small classes (maximum 18) for Common Entrance and scholarships to all major public schools. The syllabus covers and exceeds National Curriculum requirements. Those with special needs are well catered for.

Entry requirements: By interview. One bursary awarded annually at headmaster's discretion. Academic and leisure facilities set in a stimulating yet secure 80-acre estate. New classroom block, music school and refurbished chapel. Modern science block; dedicated IT, art and design departments; new indoor sports centre and sporting facilities include squash court and nine-hole golf course. Pastoral care and boarding facilities: each child is under the watchful eye of two house tutors and a form teacher; resident staff and matrons supervise boarders in comfortable dormitories. Separate girls' boarding accommodation. Nursery and pre-prep on site.

Clifton College Preparatory School,
Bristol, England
Co-ed, Boarding and Day, 8–13

Head Mr John Milne
The Avenue, Clifton
Bristol
England
BS8 3HE
T: 0117 315 7502
E: admissions@clifton-college.avon.sch.uk
W: www.cliftoncollegeuk.com

Age range 8–13; Boarding from 10
No of pupils 380; Girls 190; Boys 190
Religious denomination
    Church of England
Founded 1862
Member of BSA, CReSTeD, IAPS, ISA
Fees £14,025–£24,450

Clifton College is one of England's most famous public schools. Founded in 1862 it has always enjoyed being at the forefront of education in the UK and is superbly located in what has been described as 'the handsomest suburb in Europe', offering continuity of boarding and day education for girls and boys aged 3–18.

Day and boarding pupils mix easily together and visitors notice the happy faces, the open and friendly atmosphere and the clear sense of purpose. Clifton offers a variety of scholarships, awards and bursaries.

Academic excellence (16 to Oxbridge in 2012 and 12 places offered in 2013), superb sporting and cultural facilities, magnificent buildings, a pioneering spirit and a high level of pastoral care in a friendly community characterise Clifton in the 21st Century. Ofsted and ISI award their highest accolade of 'Outstanding' for all three Schools.

Danes Hill School, Surrey, England

Co-ed, Day only, 3–13

Headmaster Mr William Murdock
Leatherhead Road, Oxshott
Leatherhead
Surrey
England
KT22 0JG
T: 01372 842509
E: registrar@daneshillschool.co.uk
W: www.daneshillschool.co.uk

Age range 3–13
No of pupils 886; Girls 404; Boys 482
Religious denomination Christian
Founded 1947
Member of IAPS, ISBA

Danes Hill is widely recognised as one of the leading co-educational day preparatory schools in the country. Situated in 55 acres of stunning landscaped grounds in the village of Oxshott, Surrey, Danes Hill provides boys and girls aged 3–13 with a broad and balanced curriculum. Pupils are encouraged to realise their fullest academic potential and, each year, a large number of scholarship are achieved by Danes Hill pupils. Danes Hill children are characteristically self-confident and outgoing and, in addition to the emphasis on academic work, they have plenty of opportunity to develop sporting, musical, dramatic and other non-academic interests.

Our mission is to develop young people with active and creative minds, a sense of understanding and compassion for others, and the courage to act on their beliefs.

Devonshire House School, London, England

Co-ed, Day only, 2–13

Headmistress Mrs S Piper
2 Arkwright Road, Hampstead
London, England
NW3 6AE
T: 020 7435 1916
E: enquiries@devonshirehouseprepschool.
    co.uk
W: www.devonshirehouseschool.co.uk

Age range 2–13; Girls 2½–11
No of pupils 620; Girls 280; Boys 340
Religious denomination
    Non-Denominational
Founded 1989
Member of IAPS
Fees £8,025–£15,300

The school, situated in fine premises in the heart of Hampstead, aims to achieve high-academic standards whilst developing enthusiasm and initiative throughout a wide range of interests. Early literacy and numeracy are very important and traditional academic subjects form the core curriculum. Computers are used from an early age and sciences form an important part of the timetable as children grow older. Lessons are also taken in art, music, drama, French and PE. The Oak Tree Nursery takes children from 2 and a half years of age. For children entering the junior school from age three to five, places are offered following an assessment. From six; places are usually subject to a written test. Entry to the upper school is principally from the junior school. For pupils seeking to join the school from elsewhere, places are normally subject to a written entrance test.

SUBLIMIORA PETAMUS

Eagle House School, Berkshire, England
Co-ed, Day and Boarding, 3–13

Headmaster Mr Andrew Barnard	**Age range** 3–13
Crowthorne Road	**No of pupils** 361; Girls 156; Boys 205
Sandhurst	**Religious denomination** Church of
Berkshire	England
England	**Founded** 1820
GU47 8PH	**Member of** IAPS
T: 01344 772143	**Fees** £9,750–£20,850
E: info@eaglehouseschool.com	
W: www.eaglehouseschool.com	

Eagle House is a boarding and day Prep, Pre-Prep and Nursery located in beautiful grounds and with excellent facilities, we offer a rewarding education where success, confidence and happiness are paramount. As part of the Wellington College group of schools we benefit from a foundation that is pushing education to new and exciting levels. Children are central to all we do and our school is a way of life for all pupils. We unashamedly offer lots and know that busy children are happy and fulfilled children. Learning for Life means that children benefit from an all-round education. They can feel confident in the classroom, on the games field, on stage, in the concert hall and in the community. We want our children to learn and each individual is given the chance to stretch him or herself in every area.

EDGE GROVE

Edge Grove, Hertfordshire, England

Co-ed, Day and Boarding, 3–13

Headmaster Mr B Evans
Edge Grove
Aldenham Village
Hertfordshire
England
WD25 8NL
T: 01923 855724
E: office@edgegrove.com
W: www.edgegrove.com

Age range 3–13; Main entry points at 3+,
4+, 7+ and 11+.
No of pupils 352; Girls 129; Boys 223
Religious denomination Church of
England
Founded 1935
Member of BSA, IAPS, ISBA
Fees £5,985–£19,800

Outstanding support is available for the academic; extra-curricular and personal development crucial for progression. Edge Grove is a successful day and boarding school for boys and girls, characterised by a genuine commitment to the pursuit of excellence. It is situated in 28 acres of beautiful parkland where pupils are exposed to a wide range of experiences and develop confidence in a challenging and inspirational environment. With class sizes of approximately 16, Edge Grove offers academic excellence to the brightest and support to the less able. Pupils are prepared for a wide range of senior schools across the country, carefully chosen to suit their academic and extra-curricular strengths. Excellent facilities include two science labs, outdoor swimming pool, hockey pitch, tennis courts, large sports hall and outdoor cricket nets. An extensive After School Activities Programme is offered daily and on Saturday mornings.

Forres Sandle Manor, Hampshire, England

Co-ed, Boarding and Day, 3–13

FSM
Forres Sandle Manor
Independent Preparatory School

Headmaster Mr Mark Hartley
Sandleheath
Fordingbridge
Hampshire
England
SP6 1NS
T: 01425 653181
E: office@fsmschool.com
W: www.fsmschool.com

Age range 3–13
No of pupils 259; Girls 114; Boys 145
Religious denomination
    Church of England
Founded 1910
Member of BSA, IAPS
Fees £8,010–£20,970

Forres Sandle Manor (FSM) is an innovative and inspirational yet traditional country prep school set in beautiful grounds on the edge of the New Forest. Wide ability intake, however the quality of teaching is such that, year after year, they continue to have 100% success at CE along with their fair share of scholarships and awards. The Learning Centre for children who learn differently is nationally renowned. Sport and the Creative Arts also play a big part in school life. The boarding at FSM is outstanding and a strength of the school, with over 100 full and weekly boarders and waiting lists for day children wishing to convert. Visit the website to get a flavour and then make an appointment to see the Headmaster – you can be assured of a warm welcome!

Fulham Prep School, London, England

Co-ed, Day only, 4–13

FULHAM PREP SCHOOL

Principal & Head of Prep School
Mrs J Emmett
200 Greyhound Road
London
England
W14 9SD
T: 020 7386 2444
E: prepadmin@fulhamprep.co.uk
W: www.fulhamprep.co.uk

Age range 4–13
No of pupils 600; Girls 250; Boys 350
Religious denomination Non-
  Denominational
Founded 1996
Fees £13,950–£15,450

Curriculum: In the pre-prep school, the curriculum, though broadly based, lays particular emphasis on the early acquisition of the traditional basic skills of reading, writing and numeracy. We do not prepare children for 7+ and 8+ exams. The curriculum in the prep school is based on the demands of the 11+ and 13+ Common Entrance exams. Entry requirements: The school is non-selective at the Reception stage; while entry into other years is by assessment in maths and English. Siblings of current pupils are given priority. Academic and extra curricula: Academic achievement is strong but we also put a lot of emphasis on all-round development; providing an extensive range of activities featuring sport, music, art and drama. The school has two choirs and an orchestra. A wide range of lunchtime and after-school clubs is offered each term.

Gayhurst School, Buckinghamshire, England

Co-ed, Day only, 3–13

Headmaster Mr A J Sims
Bull Lane, Chalfont St Peter
Gerrards Cross
Buckinghamshire
England
SL9 8RJ
T: 01753 882690
E: gayhurst@gayhurstschool.co.uk
W: www.gayhurstschool.co.uk

Age range 3–13
No of pupils 346; Girls 43; Boys 303
Religious denomination Christian
Founded 1908
Member of AGBIS, IAPS, ISA, NAHT
Fees £9,882–£12,555

Gayhurst is a happy, thriving and vibrant co-educational, independent preparatory school for children aged 3 to 13 in Gerrards Cross, Buckinghamshire. Our girls and boys learn and flourish in our friendly, wonderfully resourced environment with small class sizes and committed, caring staff. We strive to instill confidence, a sense of decency, tolerance and sensitivity for others in our pupils. Academic standards are high and the results of external entrance examinations are outstanding at both 11+ and 13+. Opportunities outside the classroom abound. Excellent sports' facilities, first class music, art and drama encourage every child to find their own particular strengths.

Godstowe Preparatory School,

Buckinghamshire, England

Girls, Day and Boarding, 3–13

Headmaster Mr D Gainer
Shrubbery Road
High Wycombe
Buckinghamshire
England
HP13 6PR
T: 01494 529273
E: schooloffice@godstowe.org
W: www.godstowe.org

Age range 3–13; Co-ed 3–7
No of pupils 416; Girls 399; Boys 17
Religious denomination
    Church of England
Founded 1900
Member of IAPS

Godstowe is a happy and thriving preparatory school for girls aged 7 to 13, approximately a third of whom are boarders. We also have a lively Pre-Prep and Nursery for girls and boys aged 3 to 7. Godstowe is well known for setting the highest possible standards and enjoys an enviable reputation. We believe that we are the best at what we do and would very much like to have the chance to show you why we are so proud of Godstowe. Given the chance, children flourish here, in and out of the classroom. We can provide an outstanding preparation for senior school and are always mindful of the fact that just as important as what girls know will be what they are like. Enjoyment, at Godstowe, is compulsory. Don't take our word for it; come and see for yourself. You will be made to feel very welcome. David Gainer, Headmaster.

Hawkesdown House School, London, England

Boys, Day only, 3–8

Head Mrs C Bourne
27 Edge Street
Kensington
London
England
W8 7PN
T: 0207 727 9090
E: admin@hawkesdown.co.uk
W: www.hawkesdown.co.uk

Age range 3–8
No of pupils 148; Boys 148
Religious denomination
  Non-Denominational
Founded 2001
Member of IAPS, ISA
Fees £13,335–£15,270

Hawkesdown House is a unique pre-prep for boys in the heart of London's Kensington. Tucked behind Notting Hill it is equidistant from Kensington Gardens and Holland Park. The School has a single class Nursery entry 3+ and thereafter a double class entry from Reception to Year 3. The ethos of the School is to nurture the potential of each boy, finding their special talents and gifts whilst promoting happiness and a profound sense of self. The boys are encouraged to be as independent, and feel as valued as possible. School Council, a House system and open communication with the staff offer the boys many opportunities to contribute to School life. Boys are prepared for top central London day schools, including the most academically selective, and country day and boarding schools at 8+. Much emphasis is also placed on sport and music, with a wide range of options available from football, cricket, judo and fencing to class music and individual singing, violin and piano lessons.

Hazlegrove Preparatory School,
Somerset, England

Co-ed, Day and Boarding, 2–13

HAZLEGROVE

Deo Juvante

The Headmaster Mr R Fenwick
Sparkford
Somerset
England
BA22 7JA
T: 01963 440314
E: admissions@hazlegrove.co.uk
W: www.hazlegrove.co.uk

Age range 2–13
No of pupils 370; Girls 165; Boys 205
Religious denomination Church of
England
Founded 1519
Member of BSA, CReSTeD, IAPS
Fees £7,578–£21,984

Hazlegrove is set in a stunning location in the South-West and benefits from outstanding facilities – direct access to the A303 ensures journey times are minimal. Around one third of pupils aged seven and over board, enjoying a busy programme of after-school and weekend activities (Ofsted 'Outstanding'). In today's rapidly changing and demanding world, Hazlegrove believes it is important that children have a breadth of opportunity to develop their abilities and potential, while enjoying the benefit of a caring, structured and secure environment. The relationship between pupils and staff is key. Academic rigour is a priority alongside sport, music, drama, outdoor education and art with all pupils participating in every aspect of school life. The success enjoyed by pupils moving on at 13 is considerable.

Holmewood House, Kent, England

Co-ed, Day and Boarding, 3–13

Headmaster Mr J D B Marjoribanks
Barrow Lane, Langton Green
Tunbridge Wells, Kent
England
TN3 0EB
T: 01892 860006
E: registrar@holmewood.kent.sch.uk
W: www.holmewood.kent.sch.uk

Age range 3–13
No of pupils 472; Girls 206; Boys 266
Religious denomination
Inter-Denominational
Founded 1945
Member of BSA, IAPS, ISBA
Fees £4,800–£18,975

'I believe us to be the outstanding Prep School in the South-East for excellence of provision, opportunity, environment, pastoral care, personal development, family feel, purposefulness, challenge, buzz, academic expectations and fun. We offer an outstanding package for parents who want the very best for their children. We are a forward-thinking school, with an approach to education which blends the best of today's pedagogical thinking with the best of what has always worked well and does not need to change. We still teach Latin and Greek and we are considering the propitious introduction of tablets but not the variety made of stone! We are proud of our academic pedigree and not afraid to flaunt it.' A current parent recently remarked: 'Holmewood is every mother's dream!' James Marjoribanks, Headmaster.

Holmwood House Preparatory School,
Essex, England

Co-ed, Day and Boarding, 4–13

Headmaster Mr AJ Mitchell

Chitts Hill, Lexden

Colchester

Essex

England

CO3 9ST

T: 01206 574305

E: headmaster@holmwood.essex.sch.uk

W: www.holmwood.essex.sch.uk

Age range 4–13; Flexi boarding
from Year 5 & weekly boarding
from Year 6

No of pupils 360; Girls 129; Boys 231

Religious denomination
Non-Denominational

Founded 1922

Member of IAPS

Fees £8,490–£14,985

Holmwood House was founded in 1922 and stands in 34 acres of grounds only 2 km from Colchester town centre in Essex. Children of all abilities are welcomed and are prepared for the Common Entrance examination and for scholarships to senior independent schools both locally and nationally. The principal aim of the school is genuine all-round education with high academic standards at its core. Small class sizes, well-qualified staff, superb facilities and high-quality leadership ensure pupils at all levels make excellent progress. Specialist teaching starts in Reception (French, music, PE, games, swimming) and this increases by age 6/7. In the Prep school, specialist teaching in all subjects offers pupils an outstanding range and depth of curriculum. Flexi and weekly boarding are both popular options.

Millfield Prep School, Somerset, England

Co-ed, Day and Boarding, 2–13

MILLFIELD
PREP SCHOOL

Head Mrs Shirley Shayler
Glastonbury
Somerset
England
BA6 8LD
T: 01458 832446
E: admissions@millfieldprep.com
W: www.millfieldprep.com

Age range 2–13; Boarders from age 7
No of pupils 441; Girls 205; Boys 236
Religious denomination
Inter-Denominational
Founded 1945
Member of IAPS
Fees £5,730–£24,120

Millfield Prep's strength lies in the belief that every child is an individual. With world-class facilities, small class sizes and a breadth of subjects on offer, we aim to give every child the maximum opportunity to find their individual strengths and aim for excellence. Our rigorous academic programme is supported by a strong extra-curricular programme in the Arts, Drama, Music and Sport, including over 50 extra-curricular activities. Millfield is extremely proud of its international character. We believe that the rich cultural diversity provides a great opportunity for pupils and staff to learn about cultural differences. The quality of boarding is exceptional and fully supports the school's aim to provide excellent pastoral care for its pupils. The starting age for boarding is 7 years old. Our outstanding facilities include an equestrian centre, an art and design centre, music school, recital hall, golf course, 25 m indoor pool, tennis courts and a Learning Development Centre.

Notre Dame School, Surrey, England

Girls, Day only, 4–11

Headmaster Mr D Plummer
Burwood House, Convent Lane
Cobham, Surrey
England
KT11 1HA
T: 01932 869990
E: registrar@notredame.co.uk
W: www.notredame.co.uk

Age range 4–11; 2–4 BlueBelles Nursery
 Co-ed
No of pupils 715; Girls 700; Boys 15
Religious denomination Roman Catholic
Member of GSA, IAPS
Fees £1,020–£3,860

All that is best in modern society works on the sound principles of intelligence, initiative, compassion and mutual co-operation. These are the qualities you will find embedded in the ethos of Notre Dame School. When you visit Notre Dame, you will find a vibrant and successful independent school catering for pre-prep, prep and also senior pupils, which is constantly evolving and developing the quality and scope of its facilities. We are immensely proud of our peaceful grounds, fully-equipped Learning Resource Centre, capacious sports hall, nonagonal 380-seater Theatre, health and fitness studio, contemporary Sixth Form block, stunning Tree House and indoor heated swimming pool, complete with modern facilities. These, together with our healthy eating initiatives and vibrant cafeteria-style dining room, ensure our busy students have all the opportunities for a balanced lifestyle.

Papplewick, Ascot, Berkshire, England

Boys, Day and Boarding, 6–13

Head Mr T W Bunbury	**Age range** 6–13
Windsor Road	**No of pupils** 207; Boys 207
Ascot, Berkshire	**Religious denomination**
England	Church of England
SL5 7LH	**Founded** 1947
T: 01344 621488	**Member of** BSA, IAPS, ISBA
E: Registrar@papplewick.org.uk	**Fees** £13,350–£24,120
W: www.papplewick.org.uk	

Papplewick, an independent preparatory school in Ascot for boys aged 6–13, is a place where boys really can be boys. There's a hugely popular snake club, a rocket club and waveboarding at break time. Headmaster Tom Bunbury, with his many years of experience in a boys' school, believes that much of Papplewick's success comes from being an all-boys school. 'The mix of energy, empathy and academic excellence, that is unique to an all-boys' school, contributes hugely to boys' success and to their confidence when they leave school,' he says. Papplewick boys emerge extremely well equipped for the next stage, both personally and academically. The school feeds many of the UK's top independent senior schools including Eton, Harrow, Winchester, Wellington, Stowe and Bradfield.

St John's Beaumont, Berkshire, England

Boys, Boarding and Day, 3–13

Headmaster Mr G E F Delaney
Priest Hill, Old Windsor
Berkshire
England
SL4 2JN
T: 01784 432428
E: admissions@stjohnsbeaumont.co.uk
W: www.stjohnsbeaumont.org.uk

Age range 3–13
No of pupils 310; Boys 310
Religious denomination
Roman Catholic
Founded 1888
Member of IAPS, ISA
Fees £15,000–£23,700

St John's Beaumont is a Roman Catholic boys' boarding and day preparatory school in Old Windsor, 35 minutes from London. Proud of our Jesuit heritage and founded in 1888, St John's is set in 70 acres with outstanding facilities including a £3M sports centre with climbing wall, fitness suite, drama and iMac design studios. Boys are prepared for some of the country's top public schools, with many scholarships won. Alongside our day boy community, our boarding house thrives and offers the opportunity to develop a sense of confidence, independence, tolerance, friendship and respect for others. WiFi is available throughout the school and there is a strong musical tradition and excellent extra-curricular programme including polo, scuba-diving, bug club, rowing, ethics, archery, science, ecology and chess.

St Paul's Cathedral School, London, England

Co-ed, Day and Boarding, 7–13

St PAUL'S CATHEDRAL SCHOOL

Head Master Mr N R Chippington
2 New Change
London
England
EC4M 9AD
T: 020 7248 5156
E: admissions@spcs.london.sch.England
W: www.spcslondon.com

Age range 7–13
No of pupils 251; Girls 96; Boys 155
Religious denomination
  Church of England
Founded 1123
Member of AGBIS, IAPS, ISBA, NAHT
Fees £7,194–£12,435

Governed by the Dean and Chapter, the original residential choir school now includes non-chorister day boys and girls aged 4–13. A broad curriculum leads to 11+ and 13+ exams. The school has an excellent record in placing pupils in senior schools of their choice, many with scholarships. A wide variety of sports and musical instrument tuition are offered. Choristers receive an outstanding choral training as members of the renowned St Paul's Cathedral Choir. Facilities: the school has a separate Pre-Prep department, improved classrooms including a newly refurbished science lab and ICT room. There are plans to provide new boarding facilities for the choristers. Children are assessed before September entry at 4+ or 7+ years old. Voice trials for choristers are held for boys of nearly 7 years and upwards.

Stonyhurst St Mary's Hall, Lancashire, England

Co-ed, Day and Boarding, 3–13

Headmaster Mr L A Crouch
Stonyhurst
Clitheroe
Lancashire
England
BB7 9PZ
T: 01254 827073
E: admissions@stonyhurst.ac.uk
W: www.stonyhurst.ac.uk

Age range 3–13
No of pupils 205; Girls 84; Boys 121
Religious denomination Roman Catholic
Founded 1593
Member of BSA, HMC, IAPS, ISA, ISBA
Fees £6,881–£21,120

Stonyhurst St Mary's Hall is the preparatory school of Stonyhurst providing the first steps in a seamless education from age 3–18. The preparatory school is on the same site at the senior school, in its own buildings but able to take advantage of all the facilities on offer across the campus. We provide a strong sense of family and community to both our boarders and day pupils and encourage them to pursue excellence in all parts of school life. With this in mind we aim to develop the whole person. Traditional Christian values underpin everything we do as we aim to develop the whole person and give an all round education. Hodder House is our specialist department for Key Stage 1 & 2 (aged 3–7) where our younger children learn in a separate environment especially designed for them with dedicated staff.

Walhampton, Hampshire, England

Co-ed, Boarding and Day, 2–13

Headmaster Mr T Mills
Walhampton
Lymington
Hampshire
England
SO41 5ZG
T: 01590 613 300
E: office@walhampton.com
W: www.walhampton.com

Age range 2–13; Boarders from 7
No of pupils 333; Girls 154; Boys 179
Religious denomination
　Church of England
Founded 1948
Member of AGBIS, BSA, CReSTeD, IAPS
Fees £5,550–£14,985

Set within one hundred acres in the New Forest, Walhampton is a day and boarding prep school that provides a striking balance of academic rigour alongside sport, drama, art, music and over 60 on-site extra-curricular activities. A hidden gem set on the South Coast, the school has one of the ultimate prep school settings in the country. Walhampton is committed to education that offers each child true breadth and variety. Few independent prep schools offer such a range of academic and extra-curricular opportunities, from debating and general knowledge to sailing on its own lakes and riding in a professionally qualified equestrian centre. Walhampton believes in the importance of academic achievement, working with both child and parents to find the right future senior school. Parents and children are welcome to Open Mornings. The registrar can be contacted for further details on 01590 613 303 or email registrar@walhampton.com.

West Hill Park School, Hampshire, England

Co-ed, Day and Boarding, 3–13

Head Mr Alastair Ramsay
West Hill Park, Titchfield
Fareham
Hampshire
England
PO14 4BS
T: 01329 842356
E: admissions@westhillpark.com
W: www.westhillpark.com

Age range 3–13
No of pupils 250; Girls 120; Boys 130
Religious denomination
Non-Denominational
Founded 1920
Member of BSA, IAPS
Fees £9,720–£20,925

At West Hill Park School, your child will be welcomed into a happy, supportive community in which everyone is valued and where we encourage everyone to show respect and care for one another. Excellent academic performance is central to the school's ethos. However we are careful not to measure children by academic achievement alone and place real value on the breadth of experience they gain. Effort, enthusiasm and conduct are highly esteemed and the resulting growth in confidence is the key to unlocking other accomplishments. Breadth and diversity are crucial to the philosophy of West Hill Park. We encourage children to take every opportunity life brings and to appreciate the world around them. The extensive activities programme epitomises the school's attitude that children are capable of anything, if only we let them try.

PREPARATORY SCHOOLS INDEX OF GEOGRAPHIC REGIONS

The South East

Aberdour School
Surrey

Aldro School
Surrey

Ashdown House School
East Sussex

The Beacon School
Buckinghamshire

Bedales Prep School, Dunhurst
Hampshire

Brambletye
West Sussex

Brighton College Prep School
East Sussex

Caldicott School
Buckinghamshire

Cheam School
Berkshire

Claremont Fan Court School
Surrey

Copthorne Prep School
West Sussex

Cottesmore School
West Sussex

Cranleigh Preparatory School
Surrey

Cranmore School
Surrey

Cumnor House School
Surrey

Danes Hill School
Surrey

Daneshill School
Hampshire

Davenies School
Buckinghamshire

Derwent Lodge School for Girls
Kent

Downsend School
Surrey

Eagle House School
Berkshire

Edge Grove
Hertfordshire

Edgeborough
Surrey

Elstree School
Berkshire

Farleigh School
Hampshire

Forres Sandle Manor
Hampshire

Gayhurst School
Buckinghamshire

Godstowe Preparatory School
Buckinghamshire

Hall Grove School
Surrey

The Hawthorns School
Surrey

Highfield School
Hampshire

Hilden Grange School
Kent

Hilden Oaks School
Kent

Holmewood House
Kent

Holmwood House Preparatory School
Essex

Horris Hill School
Berkshire

Junior King's Canterbury
Kent

Kew Green Preparatory School
Surrey

King's House School
Surrey

King's Preparatory School
Kent

Lambrook
Berkshire

Ludgrove
Berkshire

Marlborough House School
Kent

Notre Dame School
Surrey

Papplewick, Ascot
Berkshire

The Pilgrims' School
Hampshire

Priory Preparatory School
Surrey

Rokeby School
Surrey

The Portsmouth Grammar School
Hampshire

Rose Hill School
Kent

Saint Ronan's School
Kent

Sevenoaks Preparatory School
Kent

Shrewsbury House School
Surrey

Solefield School
Kent

St Andrew's School
East Sussex

St Bede's Prep School
East Sussex

St John's Beaumont
Berkshire

St Piran's Preparatory School
Berkshire

Sunningdale School
Berkshire

Swanbourne House School
Buckinghamshire

Twyford School
Hampshire

Vinehall School
East Sussex

Walhampton
Hampshire

Wellesley House School
Kent

West Hill Park School
Hampshire

Westbourne House School
West Sussex

Windlesham House School
West Sussex

Yardley Court Preparatory School
Kent

Yateley Manor Preparatory School
Hampshire

The South West and Wales

All Hallows Preparatory School
Somerset

Badminton School
Bristol

Blundell's Preparatory School
Devon

Brabyns School
Cheshire

Chafyn Grove School
Wiltshire

Clayesmore Preparatory School
Dorset

Clifton College Preparatory School
Bristol

The Downs School
Bristol

Exeter Cathedral School
Devon

Hazlegrove Preparatory School
Somerset

Heywood Preparatory School
Wiltshire

King's Hall
Somerset

Kingswood Preparatory School
Bath & North East Somerset

Leaden Hall School
Wiltshire

Millfield Preparatory School
Somerset

Monkton Prep
Bath & North East Somerset

Mount House School
Devon

Pinewood School
Wiltshire

Port Regis Preparatory School
Dorset

Prior Park Preparatory School
Wiltshire

Queen's College Junior, Pre-Prep &
Nursery Schools
Somerset

Sandroyd School
Wiltshire

Sherborne Preparatory School
Dorset

St John's-on-the-Hill
Monmouthshire

St Michael's Preparatory School
Channel Islands

Tockington Manor School
Bristol

Terra Nova School
Cheshire

Wells Cathedral Junior School
Somerset

London

Alleyn's School
London

Garden House School
London

Arnold House School
London

Glendower Preparatory School
London

Bute House Preparatory School for
Girls
London

The Hall School
London

Cameron House School
London

Hawkesdown House School
London

Colet Court
London

Highgate School
London

Devonshire House School
London

Hill House International Junior
School
London

Dulwich College Preparatory School
London

Hornsby House School
London

Durston House
London

James Allen's Preparatory School
London

Eaton House The Manor Girls'
School
London

Kensington Prep School
London

Fulham Prep School
London

King's College Junior School
London

Latymer Prep School
London

Newton Prep
London

Northcote Lodge School
London

Notting Hill Preparatory School
London

Orley Farm School
Middlesex

Pembridge Hall
London

St Christopher's School
London

St John's Northwood
Middlesex

St Paul's Cathedral School
London

The Study Preparatory School
London

Sussex House School
London

Westminster Abbey Choir School
London

Westminster Cathedral Choir School
London

Westminster Under School
London

Wetherby Preparatory School
London

Wimbledon High School GDST
London

The Midlands and the East

Abberley Hall
Worcestershire

Beachborough School
Northamptonshire

Beaudesert Park School
Gloucestershire

Bedford Girls School
Bedfordshire

Bedford Modern School
Bedfordshire

Bedford Preparatory School
Bedfordshire

Beechwood Park School
Hertfordshire

Beeston Hall School
Norfolk

Berkhamsted School
Hertfordshire

Bilton Grange
Warwickshire

Birchfield School
West Midlands

Bishop's Stortford College Junior
School
Hertfordshire

Bromsgrove Preparatory School
Worcestershire

Cheltenham College Junior School
Gloucestershire

Christ Church Cathedral School
Oxfordshire

Dean Close Preparatory School
Gloucestershire

The Downs, Malvern
Worcestershire

Dragon School
Oxfordshire

The Elms
Worcestershire

Foremarke Hall
Derbyshire

Gresham's Prep School
Norfolk

Grosvenor School
Nottinghamshire

Haberdashers' Aske's Boys' School
Herfordshire

Hatherop Castle School
Gloucestershire

Headington School
Oxfordshire

King's College School
Cambridgeshire

Laxton Junior School
Northamptonshire

Lockers Park
Hertfordshire

Magdalen College Junior School
Oxfordshire

Maidwell Hall School
Northamptonshire

The Manor Preparatory School
Oxfordshire

Moor Park School
Shropshire

Moreton Hall Preparatory School
Suffolk

Moulsford Preparatory School
Oxfordshire

New College School
Oxfordshire

New Hall Preparatory School
Essex

Northwood Preparatory School
Hertfordshire

The Oratory Preparatory School
Oxfordshire

Orwell Park
Suffolk

Packwood Haugh School
Shropshire

The Perse School
Cambridgeshire

Prestfelde Preparatory School
Shropshire

S. Anselm's School
Derbyshire

Spratton Hall
Northamptonshire

St Faith's
Cambridgeshire

St Hugh's School
Oxfordshire

St John's College School
Cambridgeshire

Stamford Junior School
Lincolnshire

Summer Fields
Oxfordshire

Wellingborough School
Northamptonshire

Winchester House School
Northamptonshire

York House School
Hertfordshire

The North of England

Aysgarth School
North Yorkshire

The Froebelian School
West Yorkshire

Highfield Preparatory School
North Yorkshire

Malsis School
North Yorkshire

Nottingham High School for Girls
GDST
Nottinghamshire

St Martin's Ampleforth
North Yorkshire

St Olave's School
Yorkshire

Stonyhurst St Mary's Hall
Lancashire

Yarm Preparatory School
Cleveland

Scotland

Ardvreck School
Perth and Kinross

Belhaven Hill
Lothian

Cargilfield
Lothian

Craigclowan Preparatory School
Perth and Kinross

Fettes College,
Lothian

Kilgraston
Perth and Kinross

PART 3
INTERNATIONAL SCHOOLS

100

THE GABBITAS HIGHLIGHTED INTERNATIONAL SCHOOLS

Colin Bell, CEO of COBIS, introduces highlighted international schools

In this section we introduce an additional selection of international schools from around the world to provide internationally mobile and expatriate families with insight into the various options available.

British International Schools, as the name suggests, are schools with a distinctively British ethos and of course curriculum, which are found in different countries throughout the world. The traditional school terms, rather than semesters are used in many international independent schools, uniforms often closely resemble those of UK schools – climate allowing – and characteristically they provide a quality education for pupils preparing for entry to senior schools and universities worldwide. There are also schools in other countries such as Australia or New Zealand offering teaching in English and international qualifications, sometimes as well as domestic qualifications, which can be considered alongside the British International Schools.

Although there is a strong international focus in many UK schools, British International Schools are necessarily focused on actively promoting an international understanding, whilst respecting, and celebrating cultural diversity. This focus – as you would expect – very much comes with the *international* territory and is part and parcel of the educational experience to be had at these schools. Many have a truly international appeal catering for a wide variety of nationalities.

The British International School of Tokyo provides a good example of the environment one can expect with students from over 50 different nations.

Brian Christian, Principal explains that 'One third of our students are neither British nor Japanese; in particular we have large numbers of students from Continental Europe and from Australia and New Zealand. There is very much an international mindset at the school "to inspire our students to thrive as global citizens".' Students experience this '...every day and learn very quickly how to assimilate naturally with other cultures.'

Brian explains further that: 'We welcome students of all nationalities and academic abilities and provide a mutually supportive and tolerant community in which individuals are respected for who they are.'

Another good example of the type of educational atmosphere to be found, is The International School of Jakarta, which embraces *internationalism* in its ethos and culture. Simon Dennis the Principal and his teaching staff believe that 'Internationalism is a state of mind, an orientation, attitude or philosophy that values the moral development of the individual and recognises the importance of service to the world community.'

The Indonesian school is a clear example of a school which promotes a concern for world affairs and community service and develops inquiring, knowledgeable and caring young people with an intercultural understanding and respect.

Simon describes the whole school's approach as one conceived '...to promote tolerance of most things but not of intolerance. Internationalism permeates every subject and underpins all discussion, action and views, it celebrates cultural diversity and promotes international understanding and co-operation'.

The inter-continental approach is more often than not underpinned by an internationally focused curriculum. Many offer learning programmes and assessments close in content to those currently available in the UK independent sector, tailored to the needs of the international pupil. Schools generally offer IGCSEs, A levels or the International Baccalaureate (IB) taught in English as in UK independent schools, but themes of study are often influenced by the host country and are taught from a global perspective. The British International School of Cairo, for instance, provides an international education with elements of British and Egyptian culture and an English-style curriculum. Pupils at the school whether expatriate British, Anglo-Egyptian or those from Commonwealth countries, are taught Arabic from Year 1 and French from Year 3 and are examined for IGCSEs and the IB Diploma.

Wesley College illustrates a different case, although not entirely unrelated – those schools offering a dual curriculum. The Australian HMC school established in 1866, offers both the Victorian Certificate of Education (VCE), a qualification favoured by grammar schools in the country, and the International Baccalaureate (IB). This combination of qualifications allows the school to offer greater choice for domestic pupils and caters more fully for international pupils. There are many schools around the world that address the needs of international students in this way.

As well as the programmes of study and qualifications offered, there are other features of international schools worth mentioning, not least, the encouragement of self-discipline, pastoral care of the individual, and the opportunities to develop talents in a wide range of extra-curricular activities. The British School Al Khubairat, Abu Dhabi for example, has an impressive array of opportunities outside of the daily curriculum which help to introduce stretch and diversity for pupils.

'The sheer range and number of activities and events going on in and around the school on a daily basis is remarkable. From music workshops with the likes of the London Philharmonia, the Bolshoi Orchestra and world-famous pianist Lang Lang, to a lively calendar of competitive fixtures in sports such as rugby, netball, cricket, hockey and football, as well as a whole host of clubs and after-school activities, the commitment and enthusiasm shown by the students and the staff is impressive.' Explains former Principal, Paul Coakley.

There are similar opportunities at most international schools to develop pupils and to provide much needed balance. Activities often reflect those of the UK, including well-known and loved sports such as Rugby, Cricket, Polo at some, and the Duke of Edinburgh Awards scheme to name a few. The DofE award, for example, was noted by His Royal Highness the Earl of Wessex's during a visit to The Prague British School (PBS). Addressing participants of the International Award, Prince Edward made a most entertaining speech recounting his own experience of DofE expeditions and congratulated PBS on the leading role it plays in putting students forward for the award in the Czech Republic.

Senior teaching staff of international schools are often recruited from countries where English is the first language, and former heads of UK independent schools are well represented amongst them. As you would expect, teachers and school leaders are of a high calibre.

Attracted by the challenge of international careers, experienced heads are often recruited. For example, following a seven-year headship at Windermere School, Wendy Ellis spent a year completing a full-time MBA at Lancaster Management School before taking up the role of Principal at The British International School Bratislava to realise her international ambitions. Moreover, for successive generations of pupils and their families, the name Keith Pearey has been synonymous with the British School of Paris. He has spent nearly a quarter of a century at the School, more than a third of its operational history, before which he had teaching jobs in the UK and Jordan.

The parents and guardians of pupils attending British International Schools share a desire for outstanding education delivered by quality teachers, support staff and school leaders. The parent body for the majority of British International Schools often consists of people with an impressive and diverse range of backgrounds including diplomats, leaders of global corporations, royal families and representatives of international non-governmental organisations. Furthermore, a good number of high-profile families have chosen international schools throughout history, for example, Leka, Crown Prince of Albania – (born 1939) exiled from Albania and then invited back, attended *Aiglon, in Switzerland.* Similarly, some alumnae of international schools take their international experience and go on to great things. The famous French actor Christopher Lambert, who starred in both Highlander and Greystoke is, for example, an alumnus of the international school of Geneva.

Although there are many contributing factors to pupils' success, good teachers and opportunities are often highlighted. This can be seen from the views of students expected to achieve straight A grades at IGCSE or A level at The British School of Beijing this academic year.

'The best teachers inspire me and move beyond the simple curriculum and make me want to do well for myself. Smaller classes are best for this, though I've never really experienced the super competitive, very large class, model of education I'm not sure that this would be best for me. Teachers who can tell me when I'm not on the right track and help me get back are the ones that help me do the best that I can.' Randy Zhang.

Lawrence Greco, highlighted that the Global Classroom, an online community linking students with other schools around the world, was an integral ingredient in his success.

'The school giving me access to the Global Classroom has been a great inspiration for me and really lets me take what I've learned in class that bit further in my own way. I think the best teachers are the ones who are a bit strict but also let the students lead their own learning. The ones who really know each individual and what is best for them.'

For Erik Melander the teacher's who are open to new ideas are the ones who make the biggest impression on him. 'I try to be open to other people's opinions and to listen to them as well because I think that level of intellectual openness is important but it's not always easy. If the teacher knows me really well then they can often help me find a way to look at a problem or subject that works for me. I don't think everyone is the same.'

Teaching and inspiration are definitely important in bringing out the best in pupils but also important are the management administration processes provided by the senior management teams of international schools. One of the most important of these is the use of external inspection and assessment. The high standards of international schools are often maintained through meticulous inspections. The independent schools inspectorate, amongst other bodies, visits COBIS schools to assess all aspects of their provision. Inspectors consider not only the quality of teaching and learning but also the wider development of pupils against standards approved by the Department for Education (DfE) and monitored by Ofsted. Welfare, school leadership and the suitability of the school's premises and accommodation are also inspected to produce a holistic assessment from which constructive, practical feedback is provided.

For parents considering international schools there are many things to take into account and a good deal of research needs to be carried out in advance of making a final decision.

All are well advised to begin by finding out which schools are available in the area they are moving to. To make an initial *long list* one of the best indications of calibre is official recognition and quality assurance by an external body such as the Department for Education (UK) COBIS, FOBISIA, BSME, NABSS and LAHC. Membership of other organisations such as ECIS, CIS or the international branch of one of the UK Independent School Associations, eg the Headmasters' and Headmistresses' Conference (HMC) is also evidence of a school's standards.

It's important to contact schools as soon as you know that you may be moving abroad as they are often over-subscribed, and places may be limited. To secure a place at the school of your choice it is essential to make admissions enquiries early!

Careful consideration must be given to the curriculum and qualifications offered. Find out exactly which qualifications are offered, IGCSEs, IB or other and assess which best suits your son or daughter's learning style.

To assess academic standards, request to review details of examination results. In addition, it is useful to review a summary of the school's exit figures and student University destination data too. Take for example, pupils at King's College, Madrid in Tres Cantos, who received 164 offers from UK universities ranked in the top 50. 81 offers were from universities ranked in the top 20 and 38 from universities ranked in the top 10. The recent A level pass rate was 99.3 per cent and most of these pupils were awarded an A or a B grade. Almost 98 per cent of pupils taking AS level exams passed with nearly 70 per cent of those receiving an A or B grade. In the IGCSEs, 95 per cent passed with three quarters of the pupils achieving an A or B grade.

Recent inspection reports are a good source of information and can help to assess teaching, premises, curriculum and many other features. Prospectuses and websites also provide useful insight and help in getting a sense of the school community, recent activities, news and achievements.

Whilst it is not always possible, the best way to make a decision about a school is to visit, preferably with your children. Tim Roberts, Head of Secondary at the Prague British School, for example, invites all parents 'to visit PBS to see students at work and play and to experience what the school has to offer' before they take up a place.

The visit is perhaps even more important given that families may need to acclimatise and orientate themselves following relocation to a new country with perhaps a new professional role or posting to focus on as well. Parents should use the opportunity to meet the Headteacher and staff, and to get a feel for the atmosphere of a school. If you are unable to visit in person, the school may be able to put you in touch with current parents who can share their experiences and personal opinions – but if possible do visit.

The most appropriate school for one child will not necessarily be the best fit school for another, and the decision can be a difficult one. With careful research, however, parents can reassure themselves that they are sending their children to a top school with rigorous standards and a safe and secure international learning environment in which to develop, grow and excel.

SHERBORNE INTERNATIONAL

(formerly International College, Sherborne)

Co-educational, international, full boarding for students aged 11-16

EAL provision included throughout the curriculum

One-year and two-year I/GCSE programmes

Intensive summer courses and Easter I/GCSE revision courses

Designed to be the best: Established in 1977 Sherborne International is the school with an unrivalled reputation for providing the very best start to British independent education for children from overseas.

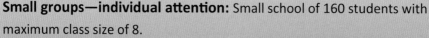

Specially trained staff: All teachers are qualified in teaching English as an Additional Language as well as their own specialist subject.

Small groups—individual attention: Small school of 160 students with maximum class size of 8.

Boarding life: In the five boarding houses experienced house parents, supported by teams of residential house tutors, provide excellent pastoral care to ensure the happiness, health and welfare of all students.

Newell Grange, Sherborne, Dorset, United Kingdom DT9 4EZ
T: +44(0)1935 814743   E: reception@sherborne-ic.net   www.sherborne-ic.net
Principal: Mrs Mary Arnal

INTERNATIONAL SCHOOLS LISTING

ⓟ = Also in Profiled Schools section

ABC International School, Vietnam
Co-ed, Day only, 2–18

Academia Britanica Cuscatleca,
El Salvador
Co-ed, Day only, 4–18

Aiglon College, Switzerland ⓟ
Co-ed, Boarding and Day, 9–18

Alexandra House School, Mauritius
Co-ed, Day only, 4–11

Alice Smith School, Malaysia
Co-ed, Day only, 3–18

Anglo-Chinese School International,
Singapore
Co-ed, Day only, 2–18

Bangkok Patana School, Thailand ⓟ
Co-ed, Day only, 2–18

Berlin British School, Germany
Co-ed, Day only, 3–18

British Embassy School Ankara,
Turkey
Co-ed, Day only, 0–14

**British International Primary School
of Stockholm**, Sweden
Co-ed, Day only, 3–12

**British International School
Belgrade**, Serbia & Montenegro
Co-ed, Day only, 4–18

**British International School
Bratislava**, Slovakia
Co-ed, Day only, 2–18

**British International School
Budapest**, Hungary
Co-ed, Day only, 3–18

The British International School Cairo, Egypt Ⓟ
Co-ed, Day only, 3–18

British International School Jakarta, Indonesia
Co-ed, Day only, 3–18

British International School of Brussels, Belgium
Co-ed, Day only, 2–11

British International School of Istanbul, Turkey
Co-ed, Day only, 2–18

The British International School of Kuala Lumpur, Malaysia
Co-ed, Day only, 3–18

British International School of Ljubljana, Slovenia Republic
Co-ed, Day only, 3–18

The British International School of New York, USA
Co-ed, Day only, 3–14

British International School of Stavanger, Norway
Co-ed, Day only, 2–16

The British International School Shanghai Pudong Campus, China
Co-ed, Day only, 1–18

British Junior Academy of Brussels, Belgium
Co-ed, Day only, 2–11

The British School – New Delhi, India
Co-ed, Day only, 3–18

The British School Al Khubairat, United Arab Emirates
Co-ed, Day only, 3–18

The British School Caracas, Venezuela
Co-ed, Day only, 3–18

British School Classic, Bulgaria
Co-ed, Day only, 4–18

British School In Baku, Azerbaijan
Co-ed, Day only, 4–18

The British School in Netherlands Senior School Voorschoten, Netherlands
Co-ed, Day only, 11–18

The British School in Tokyo, Japan
Co-ed, Day only, 3–18

The British School Kathmandu, Nepal
Co-ed, Day only, 3–18

British School of Amsterdam, Netherlands Ⓟ
Co-ed, Day only, 3–18

The British School of Beijing Shunyi Campus, China
Co-ed, Day only, 4–18

British School of Bucharest,
Romania
Co-ed, Day only, 4–18

British School of Gran Canaria,
Spain
Co-ed, Day only, 3–18

British School of Guangzhou, China
Co-ed, Day only, 3–18

British School of Houston, USA
Co-ed, Day only, 3–18

The British School of Nanjing, China
Co-ed, Day only, 4–18

The British School of Paris, France
Co-ed, Day only, 3–18

British School of Rio de Janeiro,
Brazil
Co-ed, Day only, 2–18

British School of Washington, USA
Co-ed, Day only, 3–18

The British School Quito, Ecuador
Co-ed, Day only, 3–18

Campion School Athens, Greece
Co-ed, Day only, 3–18

Colegio Anglo Colombiano,
Colombia
Co-ed, Day only, 3–18

Doha College, Qatar
Co-ed, Day only, 3–18

Doha English Speaking School,
Qatar
Co-ed, Day only, 3–11

Dubai College, United Arab Emirates
Co-ed, Day only, 11–18

Early Learning Association Primary
School, Switzerland
Co-ed, Day only, 1–12

Edron Academy (El Colegio
Britanico), Mexico
Co-ed, Day only, 2–18

The English School, Cyprus
Co-ed, Day only, 5–18

Fujairah Private Academy,
United Arab Emirates
Co-ed, Day only, 3–18

Garden International School,
Malaysia
Co-ed, Day only, 2–18

Geneva English School, Ⓟ
Switzerland
Co-ed, Day only, 3–11

The Grange School, Chile
Co-ed, Day only, 3–18

Hillcrest Secondary School, Kenya
Co-ed, Day and Boarding, 13–16

Independent Bonn International School, Germany
Co-ed, Day only, 3–11

The International School of Bangalore, India
Co-ed, Boarding and Day, 3–18

International School of Bucharest, Romania
Co-ed, Day only, 2–18

International School of Morocco, Morocco
Co-ed, Day only, 3–11

The International School of Moscow, Russia
Co-ed, Day only, 3–18

Jeddah Prep and Grammar School, Saudi Arabia
Co-ed, Day only, 2–18

Jerudong International School, Brunei Darussalam ℗
Co-ed, Day and Boarding, 2–18

Jumeirah English Speaking School, United Arab Emirates
Co-ed, Day only, 3–11

King's College, The British School of Panama, Republic of Panama
Co-ed, Day only, 3–18

King's College School, New Zealand
Co-ed, Day and Boarding, 13–18

King's College, The British School of Alicante, Spain ℗
Co-ed, Day only, 3–18

King's College Madrid, Spain
Co-ed, Day only, 2–18

King's Dubai, United Arab Emirates
Co-ed, Day only, 1–18

Kolej Tuanku Ja'Afar, Malaysia
Co-ed, Boarding and Day, 3–18

Lagos Preparatory School, ℗ Nigeria
Co-ed, Day only, 2–13

The Lancaster School, Mexico
Co-ed, Day only, 3–18

Maadi British International School, Egypt
Co-ed, Day only, 2–13

Mougins School, France ℗
Co-ed, Day only, 3–18

Oporto British School, Portugal
Co-ed, Day only, 4–18

Park Lane International School, Czech Republic
Co-ed, Day only, 3–18

Poznan British School, Poland
Co-ed, Day only, 3–14

Prague British School Kamyk, Czech
Republic
Co-ed, Day only, 4–18

Rainbow International School,
Uganda
Co-ed, Day only, 2–18

Ridley College, Canada
Co-ed, Boarding and Day, 3–18

Riverside School, Czech Republic
Co-ed, Day only, 3–18

Runnymede College, Spain
Co-ed, Day only, 3–18

Rygaards School, Denmark
Co-ed, Day only, 4–16

San Silvestre School, Peru
Co-ed, Day only, 2–18

The Sir James Henderson British
School of Milan, Italy (P)
Co-ed, Day only, 3–18

St Andrews International High
School, Malawi
Co-ed, Day only, 11–18

St Andrews International School
Sathorn, Thailand
Co-ed, Day only, 3–11

St Catherine's British School, (P)
Greece
Co-ed, Day only, 3–18

St Christopher's School, Kingdom of
Bahrain (P)
Co-ed, Day only, 3–18

St George's British International
School, Italy (P)
Co-ed, Day only, 3–18

St George's College Quilmes,
Argentina
Co-ed, Boarding and Day, 3–18

St George's College, Zimbabwe
Co-ed, Boarding and Day, 3–18

St George's International School,
Luxembourg
Co-ed, Day only, 3–18

St Hilda's College, Argentina
Co-ed, Day only, 3–18

St Michael's International School,
Japan
Co-ed, Day only, 3–11

St Paul's School, Brazil (P)
Co-ed, Day only, 3–18

St Paul's British Primary School,
Belgium
Co-ed, Day only, 3–11

Tanglin Trust School, Singapore
Co-ed, Day only, 3–18

Upper Canada College, Canada
Co-ed, Day only, 11–18

Trinity Grammar School, Australia
Co-ed, Day and Boarding, 11–18

Wesley College, Australia
Co-ed, Day only, 3–18

INTERNATIONAL PROFILED SCHOOLS

Aiglon College, Switzerland

Co-ed, Boarding and Day, 9–18

AIGLON COLLEGE
Switzerland

Head Mr Richard McDonald
61 Avenue Centrale
1885 Chesieres
Switzerland
T: +41 24 496 6161
E: info@aiglon.ch
W: www.aiglon.ch

Age range 9–18; Boarding from prep.
Latest acceptance for new students is
Lower Sixth Form.
No of pupils 340; Girls 160; Boys 180
Religious denomination
Non-Denominational
Founded 1949
Member of BSA, CIS, COBIS, HMC, IAPS,
IB, NEASC, Round
Fees CHF 54'000 – CHF 86'200

Aiglon brings together young people, ages 9 to 18, of 52 nationalities. Students study for IGCSEs, the IB Diploma as well as IELTS and SATs. Classes are taught in English. Houseparents and tutors live in eight boarding houses. The staff:pupil ratio 1:5 and the average of 8 students in each class permits the school to care for each student. Aiglon graduates gain entry to the best universities around the world. Music, drama and art occupy a prominent place in the school and there are performances during Parents' Weekend. Sports are keenly supported with a new Sports Centre and local access to a swimming pool, a skating rink, and extensive ski slopes. The school operates a unique outdoor expeditions programme. Cultural excursions are arranged to European capitals and there is a commitment to the Duke of Edinburgh's Award Scheme as well as to local and global community service projects. During summer school, for 3 or 2 weeks, students ages 9–16 take French or English classes, spend their afternoons doing outdoor activities and on weekends they go on mountain expeditions and cultural excursions.

Bangkok Patana School, Thailand

Co-ed, Day only, 2–18

Bangkok Patana School

The British International School in Thailand
Established 1957

Head Mr M Mills
643 Lasalle Road (Sukhumvit 105)
Bangna
Bangkok 10260
Thailand
T: +66 (0) 2785 2200
E: admissions@patana.ac.th
W: www.patana.ac.th

Age range 2–18
No of pupils 2239; Girls 1132; Boys 1107
Religious denomination
Non-Denominational
Founded 1957
Member of CIS, FOBISSEA, IB, NEASC
Fees THB 366,031 (approx £7,800)–THB
712,679 (approx £15,200)

Bangkok Patana School was established in 1957 to provide a British-style education to expatriate families in Bangkok. A not-for-profit organisation, it is the original British school in Thailand and is now considered one of the leading educational establishments in South East Asia. The school is proud of the distinctive accomplishments of each of its students; the outstanding teaching staff and state-of-the-art facilities ensure that students, taken from over 65 different nationalities, have maximum opportunity to fulfil their individual potential. The school's extensive extra-curricular programme emphasises a holistic approach to learning ensuring students leave not only prepared for higher education but also as well-rounded individuals ready to play their part in society.

The British International School Cairo, Egypt

Co-ed, Day only, 3–18

Head Mr S O'Grady
PO Box 137, Gezira
Cairo
Egypt
T: +202 382 0444
E: info@bisc.edu.eg
W: www.bisc.edu.eg

Age range 3–18
No of pupils 1000; Girls 550; Boys 450
Religious denomination
    Non-Denominational
Founded 1976
Member of BSME, COBIS, IAPS, IB
Fees £7,314 (sterling)–£10,710 (sterling)

The British International School, Cairo is Egypt's leading day school. It is a forward-thinking school with a progressive outlook. Academically selective, it draws its pupils from over forty nationalities. The UK National Curriculum is the platform for education up to the age of sixteen, with the IB Diploma programme in the Sixth Form. There is a rich variety of extra-curricular activities for the arts, sports, MUN, the IYA and enterprise education, supported by a significant range of events, expeditions and trips. The School has an impressive record of academic success based on high expectations of students, a very supportive parent body and high calibre teaching staff. Shared, progressive values influence the huge number of school events, such as International Week, the Christmas Bazaar and Book Week.

THE BRITISH SCHOOL OF AMSTERDAM

British School of Amsterdam, Netherlands

Co-ed, Day only, 3–18

Head Mrs J Goyer
Anthonie van Dijckstraat 1
1077 ME Amsterdam
Netherlands
T: 31 20-67 97 840
E: info@britams.nl
W: www.britams.nl

Age range 3–18
No of pupils 822; Girls 407; Boys 415
Religious denomination Non-Denominational
Founded 1978
Member of COBIS
Fees €4,938–€15,156

At the BSA we believe that education should promote a love of learning, a sense of self-worth and the worth of others, a global awareness, a sense of responsibility and a sense of wonder. Education here is focused on the individual. We work to develop inquiring, imaginative, knowledgeable and caring young people with intellectual curiosity and a sense of value. We aim to provide young people with the skills and tools they need to make informed choices in a moral context throughout their lives. We are, proudly, a non-selective school with high expectations of all. We have a strong sense of community and purpose. We provide opportunities for each child to discover and enjoy their individual talents, interests and passions. We want each child to fulfil their true potential and, most importantly, to be happy.

Geneva English School, Switzerland

Co-ed, Day only, 3–11

GENEVA
ENGLISH SCHOOL

British Education for International Children

Head Mr Stephen Baird
Route de Malagny 36, Case Postale 40
1294 Genthod
Switzerland
T: + 41 22 775 0404
E: admin@geschool.ch
W: www.geschool.ch

Age range 3–11
No of pupils 220; Girls 130; Boys 90
Founded 1961
Member of AGBIS, COBIS, FSEP
Fees CHF 22'000

Founded in 1961, Geneva English School is a happy and thriving co-educational school community set in grounds overlooking Lake Geneva for children aged 3 to 11.

We are based on the English National Curriculum but make space for French throughout the week. We are very 'British' but very 'international' too. We prepare our pupils for 11+ education in a range of local schools, as well as options back in the UK and elsewhere.

We are small enough to pay close attention not only to each child's individual academic progress but also to individual personal development. Our reputation is based on our highly talented and dedicated teachers and the unique school atmosphere. Our pupils are extremely well prepared academically and have great social confidence. The school is the first Swiss school to be accredited by the independent schools council. Geneva English School, where lifelong learning begins – where else?

Jerudong International School,

Brunei Darussalam

Co-ed, Day and boarding, 2–18

Head Mr A Fowler-Watt
PO Box 1408
Bandar Seri Begawan
BS8672
Brunei Darussalam
T: +673 241 1000
E: office@jis.edu.bn
W: www.jis.edu.bn

Age range 2–18; Boarding from Year 7
Religious denomination
Non-Denominational
No of pupils 1649; Girls 824; Boys 825
Founded 1997
Member of BSA, COBIS, FOBISIA, HMC, IAPS, IB
Fees B$7,860–B$17,688

JIS, in beautiful Brunei, set in 300 acres by the coast, is a large, thriving British International school offering an academically challenging and holistic education. The IPC, I/GCSE, A level and IB Diploma programmes are taught by some 200 highly qualified teachers. The exceptional ICT networked facilities include an Arts Centre (725 seat auditorium, dance studio, theatre and rehearsal rooms), 26 science laboratories, extensive music faculty, art, design and technology studios, libraries, traditional classrooms, swimming pool, gym, netball/basketball/tennis courts, soccer/rugby pitches. Boarding facilities are purpose designed and boarders also use the school facilities. All students and teachers are members of a House providing pastoral care, a wide range of House Events and a strong co-curricular programme exists.

King's College The British School of Alicante, Spain

Co-ed, Day only, 3–18

Head Mr D Laidlaw
Glorieta del Reino Unido 5
03008 Alicante
Spain
T: +34 96 510 6351
E: info@bsalicante.com
W: www.bsalicante.com

Age range 3–18
No of pupils 963; Girls 476; Boys 487
Religious denomination Christian
Founded 2000
Member of COBIS, NABSS
Fees €6,538–€9,057

King's College Alicante is dedicated to providing an education of the highest quality for our pupils. Children are encouraged to do their best at whatever they attempt and achieve their full potential in all areas. Our staff set the very highest standards, not only academically, but also in terms of behaviour, social skills and academic success. Our pastoral care provides support and understanding as children progress through the school and meet new challenges. Our excellent examination results for all age groups are testimony to the dedication of the staff and the endeavours of the pupils. A major strength of the school is its rich-cultural mix, with students from many different countries. Children learn to make friends and mix with people from a range of countries and cultural backgrounds.

Lagos Preparatory School, Nigeria

Co-ed, Day only, 2–13

"NON-SIBI SED OMNIBUS"

Head Mr J Samuel
36–38 Glover Road
Iyoki, Lagos
Nigeria
T: 00 234 1 740 8325
E: admin@lagosprepikoyi.com.ng
W: www.lagosprepikoyi.com

Age range 2–13
No of pupils 400; Girls 160; Boys 240
Religious denomination
Non-Denominational
Founded 2002
Member of COBIS, IAPS
Fees $6600 (£4500)–$12375 (£7800)

LPS is an International 13+ Preparatory school delivering the British National Curriculum to 400 students from 20 different nationalities. English is the medium of all tuition in this non denominational school. LPS is located in Ikoyi, the part of Lagos regarded as the prime residential area of the city. Our new purpose built premises opened in September 2010. Parents and all stakeholders have high-academic expectations and the school has a selective admissions policy. The management team are focussed on 'quality first teaching' across the whole school and this is reflected in our mission statement. The school is a member of IAPS, COBIS & AISA. LPS became the first school in the world to achieve the Every Child Matters Standards Award.

Mougins School, France

Co-ed, Day only, 3–18

Head Mr B Hickmore
615 Avenue Dr Maurice Donat
CS 12180
06252 Mougins Cédex
France
T: 00 33 (0)4 93 90 04 94
E: information@mougins-school.com
W: www.mougins-school.com

Age range 3–18
No of pupils 500; Girls 218; Boys 282
Religious denomination
Non-Denominational
Founded 1964
Member of COBIS
Fees €5,000–€16,200

Mougins School is an international school following the British curriculum and open to students aged 3–18. Academically strong, sport, music, art and theatre are also an integral part of the programme. The School's philosophy is designed to encourage students in all realms of their development and believes that pupils learn best when they are encouraged, valued, trusted and respected. An active PTA assures social activities for parents and students alike, as well as dynamic fund-raising and humanitarian work. Pastoral care for new families to assist with the hurdles of relocation is readily available.

The Sir James Henderson British School of Milan, Italy

Co-ed, Day only, 3–18

Head Dr C Ferrario
Via Carlo Alberto Pisani Dossi, 16
20134 Milan
Italy
T: +39 02 210 94 1
E: info@sjhschool.com
W: www.sjhschool.com

Age range 3–18
No of pupils 655; Girls 330; Boys 325
Founded 1969
Member of AGBIS, COBIS, HMC, IB
Fees €11,340–€18,650

The Sir James Henderson British School of Milan (SJHS) is one of the leading British schools in Italy, serving the needs of a broad international community with students of more than forty nationalities. The School follows the English National curriculum with students sitting GCSEs at age 16 and the IB at age 18. The School's Mission is to ensure that its diverse student body grows to its full potential as independent learners in a caring British and international community, uniting the best of British educational tradition with the values, practices and beliefs of the International Baccalaureate. The School promotes a holistic education. The co-curricular programme includes sport, drama, music and arts promoting self-confidence and successful academic outcomes.

St Catherine's British School, Greece

Co-ed, Day only, 3–18

Head Mr S Smith
PO Box 51019
Kifissia 14510
Greece
T: 00 30 210 2829750
E: headmaster@stcatherines.gr
W: www.st-catherines.gr

Age range 3–18;
No of pupils 1060; Girls 563; Boys 497
Religious denomination Christian
Member of AGBIS, COBIS, HMC, IB, ISBA
Fees €8,050–€13,040

St Catherine's British Embassy School was set up in 1956 for the education of British and Commonwealth children in Greece. Today there are students from 52 nationalities although priority is still given to British and Commonwealth children. Renamed St Catherine's British School from September 2012 we teach the English National Curriculum from Early Years through to the end of Key Stage 4. In Years 10 and 11 students study for the Cambridge IGSCE examinations and in Years 12 and 13 they study the International Baccalaureate Diploma. Greek, French, German and Spanish are offered at various stages. There is a strong tradition of music, drama, dance and sport. In addition to a programme of some 30 extra-curricular activities per week, the school offers the International Award Scheme and LAMDA examinations.

St Christopher's School, Kingdom of Bahrain

Co-ed, Day only, 3–18

Head Mr E Goodwin
PO Box 32052
Isa Town
Kingdom of Bahrain
T: +973 1759 8600
E: admissions.school@st-chris.net
W: www.st-chris.net

Age range 3–18
No of pupils 2135; Girls 1073; Boys 1062
Religious denomination
   Non-Denominational
Founded 1961
Member of BSME, HMC, IAPS, IB
Fees BD 2,631 (Nursery) – BD 6,906
   (Years 12 and 13)

St Christopher's first opened in 1961 and has grown to become an internationally renowned school with over 2100 students from around 70 nations. With a consistent record of excellent academic success, we also offer a broad programme of extracurricular activities and personal development opportunities. The school has been rated 'Outstanding' in 3 different inspection regimes – not just overall, but for every aspect of performance. Widely recognised as one of the world's top British schools overseas, with exceptional facilities and resources, St Christopher's is not for profit. All income from fees is used to run and further develop the School for the benefit of our students, making us the premier choice for those parents who need and demand the very best British style education for their children in Bahrain.

St George's British International School, Italy

Co-ed, Day only, 3–18

Head Mr M Hales
Via Cassia Km 16
La Storta
00123 Rome
Italy
T: 0039 06 308 6001
E: secretary@stgeorge.school.it
W: www.stgeorge.school.it

Age range 3–18
No of pupils 820; Girls 392; Boys 428
Founded 1958
Member of AGBIS, CIS, COBIS, HMC, IB
Fees €11,720–€18,570

St George's British International school is an HMC co-educational day school founded in 1958, located north of Rome in a spacious 14-acre site. It shadows the national curriculum from the Early Years programme through the Key Stages to (I)GCSE. In the Sixth Form, all pupils follow the International Baccalaureate (IB) Diploma programme. St George's is genuinely international in flavour and has pupils from over 65 nationalities. The school has a deserved reputation as one of the leading international schools of the world, achieving a 100% IB diploma pass rate in 2013, with an average score of 35. Alumni of the school are currently studying at Oxford, Cambridge, UCL, Imperial, and Edinburgh, at Yale, MIT, Berkeley, McGill, amongst other top universities around the world. Learning facilities include fully-equipped classrooms, science laboratories, IT rooms. The library contains the latest research information systems and sports facilities are extensive. Early application is recommended.

St Paul's School, Brazil

Co-ed, Day only, 3–18

Head Mr C Rowe
Rua Juquia 166, Jardim Paulistano
Sao Paulo
Brazil
01440 903
T: +55 11 3087-3399
E: head@stpauls.br
W: www.stpauls.br

Age range 3–18
No of pupils 1072; Girls 531; Boys 541
Founded 1926
Member of COBIS, HMC, IAPS, IB
Fees R$48,564–R$69,024

St Paul's School is one of the leading British schools in South America, and combines a great historical tradition of almost 90 years. Located in the prestigious borough called the Jardins, which is a residential, green and low rise area. 75% of pupils are Brazilian, with 10% British and Commonwealth. The size of the teaching staff is 160, with around 40 teachers from the UK. The Pre-Prep (ages 3–6) has 220 pupils and the Prep (6–11) 400 pupils. They follow the International Primary Curriculum, linked to the England National Curriculum. The Senior School (11–18) with 450 pupils prepares for IGCSEs and the IB in the Sixth Form. Leavers go to the best universities in the UK, Europe, the USA, Canada and Brazil. A new underground Sports Centre was opened in 2013, with swimming pool, basketball and volleyball courts.

INTERNATIONAL SCHOOLS INDEX OF GEOGRAPHIC REGIONS

Europe and The Former Soviet Union

Aiglon College
Switzerland

Berlin British School
Germany

British Embassy School Ankara
Turkey

British International Primary School
of Stockholm
Sweden

British International School
Belgrade
Serbia & Montenegro

British International School
Bratislava
Slovakia

British International School
Budapest
Hungary

British International School of
Brussels
Belgium

British International School of
Istanbul
Turkey

British International School of
Ljubljana
Slovenia Republic

British International School of
Stavanger
Norway

British Junior Academy of Brussels
Belgium

British School Classic
Bulgaria

British School In Baku
Azerbaijan

The British School in Netherlands
Senior School Voorschoten
Netherlands

British School of Amsterdam
Netherlands

British School of Bucharest
Romania

British School of Gran Canaria
Spain

The British School of Paris
France

Campion School Athens
Greece

Early Learning Association Primary
School
Switzerland

The English School
Cyprus

Geneva English School
Switzerland

Independent Bonn International
School
Germany

International School of Bucharest
Romania

The International School of Moscow
Russia

King's College Madrid
Spain

King's College, The British School
of Alicante
Spain

Mougins School
France

Oporto British School
Portugal

Park Lane International School
Czech Republic

Poznan British School
Poland

Prague British School Kamyk
Czech Republic

Riverside School
Czech Republic

Runnymede College
Spain

Rygaards School
Denmark

The Sir James Henderson British
School of Milan
Italy

St Catherine British School
Greece

St George's British International
School
Italy

St George's International School
Luxembourg

St Paul's British Primary School
Belgium

The Americas

Academia Britanica Cuscatleca
El Salvador

The British International School of
New York
USA

The British School Caracas
Venezuela

British School of Houston
USA

The British School Quito
Ecuador

British School of Rio de Janeiro
Brazil

British School of Washington
USA

Colegio Anglo Colombiano
Colombia

Edron Academy (El Colegio
Britanico)
Mexico

The Grange School
Chile

King's College, The British School
of Panama
Republic of Panama

The Lancaster School
Mexico

Ridley College
Canada

San Silvestre School
Peru

St George's College Quilmes
Argentina

St Hilda's College
Argentina

St Paul's School
Brazil

Upper Canada College
Canada

The Far East, India and Oceania

ABC International School
Vietnam

Alice Smith School
Malaysia

Anglo-Chinese School International
Singapore

Bangkok Patana School
Thailand

British International School Jakarta
Indonesia

The British International School of
Kuala Lumpur
Malaysia

The British International School
Shanghai Pudong Campus
China

The British School - New Delhi
India

The British School in Tokyo
Japan

The British School Kathmandu
Nepal

The British School of Beijing Shunyi
Campus
China

British School of Guangzhou
China

The British School of Nanjing
China

Garden International School
Malaysia

The International School of
Bangalore
India

Jerudong International School
Brunei Darussalam

King's College School
New Zealand

Kolej Tuanku Ja'Afar
Malaysia

St Andrews International School
Sathorn
Thailand

St Michael's International School
Japan

Tanglin Trust School
Singapore

Trinity Grammar School
Australia

Wesley College
Australia

The Middle East and Africa

Alexandra House School
Mauritius

The British International School
Cairo
Egypt

The British School Al Khubairat
United Arab Emirates

Doha College
Qatar

Doha English Speaking School
Qatar

Dubai College
United Arab Emirates

Fujairah Private Academy
United Arab Emirates

Hillcrest Secondary School
Kenya

International School of Morocco
Morocco

Jeddah Prep and Grammar School
Saudi Arabia

Jumeirah English Speaking School
United Arab Emirates

Kings' Dubai
United Arab Emirates

Lagos Preparatory School
Nigeria

Maadi British International School
Egypt

Rainbow International School
Uganda

St Andrews International High
School
Malawi

St Christopher's School
Kingdom of Bahrain

St George's College
Zimbabwe

GLOSSARY OF MEMBERSHIP ABBREVIATIONS

AGBIS	Association of Governing Bodies of Independent Schools
AHIS	Association of Heads of Independent Schools
BAISC	The British Association of International Schools and Colleges
BSA	Boarding Schools Association
CIS	Council of International Schools
COBIS	Council of British International Schools
CReSTeD	Council for the Registration of Schools Teaching Dyslexic Pupils
FOBISIA	The Federation of British International Schools in Asia
FSEP	Swiss Federation of Private Schools
GDST	Girls' Day School Trust
GSA	Girls' School Association
HAS	Head Teachers' Association
HMC	The Headmasters' and Headmistresses' Conference
IAPS	The Independent Association of Prep Schools
IB	International Baccalaureate
IBSCA	International Baccalaureate Schools and Colleges Association
ISA	Independent Schools Association
ISBA	Independent Schools Bursars' Associations
NABSS	National Association of British Schools in Spain
NAHT	National association of Head Teachers
NAIS	National Association of Independent Schools
NEASC	New England Association of Schools and Colleges
Round	Round Square
SCIS	Scottish Council of Independent Schools
SHMIS	Society of Headmasters and Headmistresses of Independent Schools

MAIN INDEX